THE MYTH OF ADAM AND EVE AND THE ENDURANCE OF CHRISTIANITY IN THE WEST

– A MATTER OF INTERPRETATION.

RAFAEL PINTOS-LÓPEZ

CONTENTS

Dedications — vii

1. Introduction — 1
2. The Torah — 7
3. Myth — 15
4. New Zealand and Rome — 18
5. The Myth of Adam & Eve — 20
6. Awareness of mortality — 31
7. The mystery of Cain's wife — 33
8. How humanity spread among the hominins — 36
9. Christian interpretation of the Book of Genesis — 41
10. Humans as primates — 51
11. The immortal soul — 56
12. Christianity and Judaism — 60
13. St John the Baptist — 62
14. Jesus — 66
15. St Paul — 76
16. Did we need a human god? — 86
17. Arianism, the Council of Nicaea and the Deification of Jesus — 94
18. Constantine and the Council of Nicea — 97
19. Individuality & the Church — 103
20. Martin Luther and the individual — 107
21. Possible changes in Christianity — 109
22. Scientism — 111
23. Darwin and the Evolution of the Species — 124
24. Agnosticism — 130
25. Losing my religion: the impact of a TV clip — 143
26. The West — 145
27. Christianity, the individual and the West — 148
28. God as a possibility — 163

Afterword	167
The Holy Spirit	173
Acknowledgments	175
Index	177
Notes	187

"Long persuaded of the privileged dynamism of Western ways, of the presumably unique factor of iconoclasm and futurism operative in Western science and technology, we are now experiencing a subtle counter-current, a new understanding of our confinement within ancient bounds of mental habit. We too are creatures of fable and recursive dreams" – **George Steiner**

*To Inés who, one Winter
put up with being woken up at
four o'clock in the morning
to be told the urgent news
that Adam & Eve had been hominins
who had acquired consciousness.*

*To my sons,
Hernán, Rodrigo and Millán,
three of the people
I admire the most.*

INTRODUCTION

In this book I only wish to offer a different historical perspective within the discussion among materialists and scientists on the one hand, and Christians and agnostics on the other. Up until now, the environment of the discussion has always been that relativism, acceptance, inclusiveness, and logic are all attributes of the atheists, whereas a totalitarian, hegemonic culture is exclusive to the religious group.

The object is to seek a logical reconciliation between the parties, but a true reconciliation, one that would include the post modern reality of today and the need of the deity that humanity has demonstrated throughout history.

What the book suggests is a bit what Max Weber proposed (a theory that I recognise was superseded many years ago), that the West without Christianity would not have existed, but that would include the concept that Christianity, in a new and probable re-encarnation, would take an important role in the destiny of humanity. I also propose that the West, as we know it, originated in Christianity from its very beginning, not with Protestantism but, more than anything with St Paul. Moreover, the different Protestant denominations, because of their historical circumstances, were always more exclusive and their theologies were less universalist and less synchretic than Catholicism (which called itself "universal"—that is, "Catholic" —accepted Gentiles almost from its inception, and always based itself on Judaism). The book includes other positions that are possibly more debatable, such as declaring that science and Christianity are part of the same paradigm. We accept that they are opposite poles of it, but they are still an essential part of the Western philosophical model. What the extremist debate keeps hidden is the fact that convergence is possible and that it actually exists. The pendulum, as it goes from one end to the other, passes inexorably through the middle.

The Bible offers possibilities of reassessing religion in contemporary, post modern terms. Another concept, perhaps already noticeable, is that the secularisation of the West is due, mostly, to its undeniably Christian foundation. Christianity and secularisation are complementary elements in a historical process. As secularisation advances Christianity gives way to it, slowly but surely; and it gives way in a fashion that appears predestined. Although rationalism tends to deny it, the book suggests, *inter alia*, that Christianity is possibly the religion through which organised religion could be abandoned.

But there is much more. The book bases itself on a hermeneutical examination of the Bible, not so much an exegesis, or a theological analysis, but on a logical interpretation of several facts—historical or that appear in the Old Testament or the Jewish Bible— that can only be understood from a logical, rational point of view. The book propounds ideas on the basis of those concepts.

The facts are:

1. The Judaism of the Temple—the original Jewish religion, the one of Moses and Abraham— was an archaic, natural religion, like others, with the exception that it was a monotheistic one. It had no heaven or hell. The Hebrews, like many primitive peoples, did not consider themselves superior to other animals or separated from them. When they died, they returned to the dust. That was all. They understood that they have consciousness and that, at some point in time, that must have appeared for them to become human beings. Consciousness—they knew— was the only difference between them and the rest of the animal kingdom. Judaism appeared as a religion for a nation of illiterate peasants that possessed no concept of afterlife. When I say they were illiterate I do not mean it as something derogatory, that is a fact that has been proved by archaeology: many centuries passed, after the mythical appearance of their forebears, for the Hebrews to learn how to read and write. It has also been historically proved that they did not have a concept of afterlife. Rabbinical Judaism, the descendant of the original Judaism, does not accept any afterlife, and if it somehow accepts it, it is because of the influence of Christianity. As I explain below, in those days, the aim of primitive natural religions was to defend the believer against any evil. God would give the person protection against poor harvests, enemy armies, robbers, unrequited love, foxes, the mysterious

death of some sheep, etc. Of course, those religions also provided legal as well as social and political principles. The morals of a nation passed through its religion. In that sense, the Judaism of the Temple contributed a lot to the development of the Hebrew nation.

2. The *Tanach*, or Hebrew Bible was originally written, compiled, or transcribed, if you like, in the 8th century BC, in circumstances I explain a little later. The way St Paul interpreted Hebrew mythology and the *Torah* (the first five books of the Jewish Bible) was something totally revolutionary which had totally unexpected results. It explained the violent nature of archaic religions. Sacrifice was the only way (maybe homeopathic) in which violence, human as well as divine, could be prevented. The believer killed an innocent animal or human being to satisfy a god, obtain a favour, or simply to ask for forgiveness for something they had done. Humanising a god—an all-powerful being— and killing him, turning him into the victim of a sacrifice, highlighted historical incongruities and originated the opposite process, that is, it deified not only Jesus of Nazareth, but a also a human being, bringing him closer to God the Father; prioritised the individual, with their rights and freedoms, that had to be protected; and opened the doors to a new ethic: the Western ethic. The origin of Christianity with St Paul provided a turning point, if you like, between violent religion and a religion characterised by the rights of individuals. The meeting between Meso and North American—Aztec and Maya— religions and Christianity demonstrated that. The death of Jesus resulted then in the existence of a West

that cannot accept the concept of "victim" and even less that of "human victim".
3. The beginning of the process lies—from my humble point of view—in the myth of Adam and Eve and its Christian re-interpretation (although that myth, among many, represents a Christian retrofit that ended up hiding the original ideas). The Hebrews, who probably intuited human evolution in a proto-Darwinian manner, explained the origins of humanity as something mono-genetic: a couple of primates, among many, who begin to experience consciousness. My interpretation, a quasi historical-scientific one, is based on the fact that, if we fail to interpret the myth the way I see it, many paragraphs of the Old Testament end up making no sense at all.

The Pauline re-interpretation of the Myth of Eden, far from respecting the spirit of the Hebrew Myth, retrofitted notions such as the individual immortal soul, the original sin, the Devil, Heaven and Hell, Jesus as the Son of God, etc.

Maybe it would be useful to understand that Paul needed to grow a peripheral sect of Judaism into a new universal religion. That new religion had to be based on Hebrew institutions, accepted by many for centuries. His proselytising program began with Jews and then followed with Gentiles. The acceptance of Gentiles resulted in a backlash within the sect but Paul ended up building a bridge that would historically unite both religions. Christianity chose to be an evolution of Judaism, more universal, with a higher spirituality (that is, it included the new concept of the afterlife); and with a dogma based on the teachings of Jesus of Nazareth, but without forgetting its origins. The Christian Bible includes a large part of the *Tanach*, which the Christians know as the Old Testament.

In summary, among the original ideas that appear here, the book suggests that: 1) in the Hebrew myth, Adam and Eve were a couple of hominins, pretty much like any of the human ancestors we have discovered lately; 2) the Hebrews had a much more sophisticated and realistic idea of evolution than what is believed nowadays, and that explains many points in the Bible that had no explanation until now; 3) the innovation of the Greek concept of spirit (*psyche*) introduced by St Paul when he interpreted the Book of Genesis resulted in a new self-perception of the individual (*esse est percipi*) that changed forever the course of history, because when he misinterpreted or misrepresented the *Tanach*, he spiritualised and separated humanity from the rest of the animal kingdom.

The new concept that believers acquired about themselves—which converted them in quasi-divine beings—contributed to the creation of a Christian West with a potential for growth far superior to the rest of the world.

That modern individualism, capitalism, democratic and international institutions, globalisation, free market, civil rights and atheism—i.e., the West— originated from the mix of Hellenistic ideas and Jewish culture spread by Christianity may seem something unbelievable or not very probable. As I stated before, it's all a matter of interpretation.

THE TORAH

NEITHER GOD NOR MOSES?

Currently, reading and writing are linguistic skills that are acquired after listening and speaking. They are something as natural for children as walking, using a computer, watching television or using a cell phone.

In the eyes of pre-literacy nations that were still in development, such as the Hebrews of the 8th century BC, reading and writing had numinous powers. Without a doubt, they were gifts from God, which included powers of blessing and cursing. Only kings and priests had access to them. To watch people using those skills would cause some kind of religious awe.

Let us imagine an Assyrian peasant... Locusts had had a feast in his small farm near the city of Ashur, in Assyria, and young Banistar had lost almost all of his crop. All he could think of was asking his neighbour to see if he had any more seeds. The neighbour didn't have any seeds left, but he suggested asking the priest. The priest had several pots with seeds and could lend Banistar a pot so that he could re-plant again before the following year. He had to return the seeds and make a donation to the temple. But the fantastic thing was that, as he did it, the priest took a small cane and a piece of fresh clay. He marked the clay several times with the cane. That action Banistar had witnessed for the first time, totally and literally unintelligible for him, was the miracle of writing. The priest had created a document on which the loan and Banistar's liability had been recorded and that the priest would be able to consult later on. Assyrian troops would take writing with them to every corner of their empire, including Palestine.

Writing—Hebrew, Assyrian or from wherever— would become something of paramount importance for the subjects we'll be dealing with.

The *Torah*, the Jewish Bible, was edited or compiled, if you like, under strange circumstances. Its first book is the *Torah*. *Torah* means *The Teaching* or *The Law*, and it is also called *The Pentateuch* or *The Five Books of Moses*. According to some claims it was written by God himself. Others say it was written by Moses. Even for people with inflexible religious beliefs, that may be a bit of an exaggeration. In Moses' case, if he ever existed, much of the story the *Tanach* tells occurred after his death. That belief, then, is devoid of any logic. In God's case, whoever says He wrote it should prove first that God exists and then determine when he wrote it.

What is undeniable is that the *Tanach* exists. It actually is very similar, almost identical to the Old Testament of the Christian Bible.

THE MYTH OF ADAM AND EVE AND THE ENDU...	9

At the time of writing the *Tanach*, most Hebrews were illiterate. There was no writing in Judah at least until the 8th century BC. There are no recorded cases of written Hebrew anywhere before then. That proves that even if God had written the Ten Commandments with His finger, no Jew of the time would have been able to read them (maybe Moses, and that, only if God had written them in Egyptian, as Hebrew was not a written language at that stage).

The *Torah* is in all probability a collection of myths and traditions of the Hebrews, and many parts of it were arguably compiled or edited as an indirect result of the advance of the Assyrian Empire on the northern kingdom of Israel in the 8th century BC.

After many centuries in Canaan, the Hebrews had gone from a period of power and unity, under David and later Solomon, to a period when they were divided into two weaker kingdoms, Israel, to the North, and Judah, to the South.

When Solomon died, his son Rehoboam became the king. For some reason, he raised taxes and worked his subjects very hard. He was so unpopular that ten (!) of the twelve tribes decided to secede and form a separate kingdom, Israel, under a new king called Jeroboam. There was a lot of enmity and resentment after secession. Judah, a much smaller kingdom, claimed legitimacy, as its king was descended from the House of David whereas Jeroboam was not. During the seventeen years of Jeroboam's reign both kingdoms fought often and bitterly.

Israel's location, to the south of today's Lebanon, with rich agricultural land and sea ports, the river Jordan on the eastern side, and being right in the middle of important trade routes, was too much of a temptation for the powerful Assyrians, its northern neighbours.

Assyria had been growing for some time under Shalmaneser III. Israel, much smaller and weaker, had entered into an agreement of vassalage with Assyria. Years later, in 732 BC, the Assyrians took over territories that were west of their kingdom, from the Euphrates to the Mediterranean Sea. This, more than a mere agreement of servitude was a partial occupation, and it meant that the northern Jewish kingdom had actually become much smaller, a rump state. Many Israelites from the occupied lands were resettled. As part of the policy of their occupation, the Assyrians imposed the use of the Aramaic language on all their conquered peoples. Aramaic was a lingua franca easy to speak and write, as it had alphabetic writing. This was good for the administration of their new lands. It was much easier than trying to impose their own language, Akkadian, with its complex cuneiform writing. The Hebrews began to read and write in Aramaic.

The excuse for the invasion was that Ahaz, the King of Judah at the time, who was also a vassal, had asked the Assyrian King to invade Israel, as he had felt threatened by Israel and Damascus.

Ten years later, in 722 BC, Israel would rebel against the Assyrian occupation. The move had dire consequences. The Assyrians were harsh overlords. During the previous invasion, Samaria, the capital, had been spared, but this time they occupied Samaria as well. Exactly as it had happened ten years before, the Israelites who could not escape were forcibly resettled to other parts of the empire and became what is now known as the Lost Tribes of Israel. Many of them actually escaped to Judah.

The Kingdom of Judah was spared by the Assyrians and remained independent for a short while.

The aim of the King of Judah, Hezekiah, was to recreate the 'golden age' of David and Solomon, when both Jewish kingdoms had been united. Unfortunately, Hezekiah, with his dream of a powerful Jewish nation, also led an ill-fated coalition against the Assyrians. The result was that, in 701 BC, Assyria invaded Judah as well. They failed in their attempt to take its capital, Jerusalem, but totally devastated the countryside.

Hezekiah was left with more problems than before: his kingdom had been reduced in size and much of it had been destroyed. Jerusalem was now a large city, having received the first wave of refugees from Israel and then, the second wave from what was left of it, mostly from its capital, Samaria. People had to be kept occupied and had to be fed. With so many refugees, law and order became an important issue for Judah.

This was a time of change in Judah. In the 8th century BC the kingdom had a very basic iron-age economy, olives and sheep being its most important products. In those days, the vast majority of the population was illiterate. Only some priests, scribes, and other members of the elite could read and write. Inscriptions on stele and monuments were beginning to appear but, in general, Judah's society operated in a pre-literate, primitive environment.

Hezekiah was still keen to restore the mythical "golden age". Those were the only days when the Hebrews had been united and were powerful. And when we say mythical it is not because it had not occurred. Quite probably, two or three centuries later, when things had become really bad and the only thing that was left was Jerusalem and the devastated land that surrounded it, that period looked much more golden than it actually was.

Hezekiah needed a history to be proud of. He also needed to impose the rule of law in Jerusalem and what remained of his country. Perhaps he could do both: restore pride and have a corpus of law, in one audacious move. A written collection of the traditions of the Hebrews would go a long way to instil pride in his beleaguered nation. A legal code would also help bring back the rule of law in the country. The book would include the Commandments of God and the Leviticus, which were the legal principles all Hebrews had to abide by.

Until then, all of the traditions of the Jewish nation had been transmitted orally. The Hebrews had had an oral culture going back approximately 3,000 years. With time, most of the myths and traditions had become unreal, exaggerated, embellished by repetition. For instance, Samson, one of the chieftains that had been the leaders (Judges) before the kings, was said to have been so strong that he demolished a temple. He grabbed the columns and broke them with his bare hands. Joshua had won the battle of Jericho by having his trumpeters sound their trumpets so hard that the walls that protected the town had collapsed, and so on and so forth. One thing that is important to understand is that those stories were quite believable in that day and age.

Hezekiah's ambitious project was to gather all those oral traditions. He needed the traditions in a unified set of scrolls of what would later become Scripture.

Oral tradition had been, until then, the way the nation had maintained its cultural continuity. Each generation passed their folktales and proverbs, in songs, around campfires and at home. Again, in a population of illiterate shepherds and farmers, writing would have lent prestige to those traditions because only the elite could write. Writing was the word of the State. It was also God-given.

In terms of the Law, there had been codes before —long before— Hezekiah's time. One thousand years before him, Hammurabi, King of Babylon, had based the authority of his famous Code on the fact that he worshipped the Babylonian god, Marduk: "*Hammurabi is a ruler who is as a father to his subjects, who holds the words of Marduk in reverence, who has achieved conquest for Marduk over the north and south, who rejoices the heart of Marduk, his lord, who has bestowed benefits for ever and ever on his subjects, and has established order in the land*".

Hezekiah, who on all accounts appears to have been a righteous king, found himself in the same situation as his code-writing predecessors. He was widely respected, but that was not enough for a corpus of law, history and religion as comprehensive as what this king had in mind. The scribes who compiled the histories of the *Torah* had to trace the origins of its authority to the very beginning. They could have begun with the origins of the Jews, but they chose to start with the universe and God himself, hence the Book of Genesis. The history of the Hebrews had to begin with the creation of the world and the creation of humanity. And it made sense that it be followed by Exodus and Leviticus: the way the Hebrews had arrived in Canaan from Egypt, after a long period of enslavement, and the moral principles that had been given to them by God himself.

As we have said, Hezekiah had found himself in the middle of a crisis that required, among other things, something akin to a code of law. It was not to be an actual code of law, but a mixture of history, law, tradition, a constitution, etc. His justice would be based on it. But the project was more ambitious than that. The book had to be also a pivotal element in the management of the nation and a central source of authority for the Temple.

There are many repetitions in the *Torah* or *Pentateuch*; there are stories that do not make a lot of sense to us in this day and age, and many that overlap, as you would expect from a collection of traditions that were transmitted since time immemorial and that were gathered not just during Hezekiah's reign but over a period that commenced long time before and continued for centuries. The authors of the *Torah* did a fine job of stitching the whole collection together and they came up with a very credible (for 8th century BC standards at least) account of the origins of the Jewish nation, and of the human species, from the dawn of human consciousness.

So, what history tells us is that the purpose behind the creation of the *Torah* was manifold: religious, ethical, moral, legal and political. And it served its purpose, even in ways that Hezekiah and his scribes could never have imagined. Time passed, and the interpretation of the *Torah* —the first five books of the Old Testament of the Christians— became more literal. Its collection of stories became the word of God and the foundation of the three most important religions. It also provided the basis for European culture and for Western civilisation in general.

MYTH

*W*e should try and understand that a very important part of what I will write about here is that gossamer layer of imagination that lies between fiction and some kind of suspected reality, a would-be reality. A story that becomes fiction-reality. That is what we call a myth. In this case, a myth that, generally, Christians and Jews take as a quasi-reality. Here I try to determine why people believe what they believe in; if the Torah and the Old Testament give different versions of the same episode; and if those versions are different, why are they so. This book, then, has a lot to do with a myth, in this case the myth of the creation of humanity and its consequences for people who take it one version or the other as dogma. Through this example, St Paul's task at the beginning of Christianity becomes something evident and transcendental.

Again, it is important to understand that this is where story and reality meet: Adam and Eve in the Garden of Eden, as imagined by Hebrews and interpreted by Christians, creating thus the origins of the Judaeo-Christian tradition eight centuries later.

Are the Hebrew myth and the Christian myth one and the same? Did it change? Was there a misinterpretation or a misrepresentation? This is what we discuss here.

Myth is often the explanation we make up for an event that took place so long ago that our collective memory has forgotten it or almost forgotten it. When we don't know the origin of a reality we normally create a story that explains this reality.

It's also about how real people can create a story and how that story can shape reality, even thousands of years later. Inasmuch as the story explains how reality developed, it is of the utmost importance.

At the beginning of the 20th century, in *The Protestant ethic and the spirit of capitalism*, Max Weber came up with the notion that the event that had originated the capitalist system was the Reformation. It was a well-thought concept, with a fairly logical basis, although by now it has been refuted and disproved a few times.

More than one hundred years later I am asking myself if Western civilisation is not largely based on a much older event, the Hebrew myth of Adam and Eve, or the moment St Paul retrofitted the Christian concept of the 'individual immortal soul' onto it (a real anachronism, like making the Flintstones celebrate Christmas). This is such a farfetched, incredible, notion that my instinct tells me it must have been something very important at the time. And also much, much later. Even now.

Stephen Greenblatt places the idea of the myth right next to the uncertainty of the times in which we live. Everything is unsure about these times in the West, hence the relevance of the myth: *"Perhaps the telling of an origin story is a symptom of uneasiness we attempt to calm ourselves by telling a story. Or perhaps our species somehow got ahead of itself, having taken, quite by accident, a developmental turn that led us along a path we cannot entirely understand and that provokes our speculative storytelling intelligence."* [1] I totally agree. The way things have developed after Christianity interpreted the Myth of Paradise seems to have been something totally unexpected, something serendipitous.

There are different myths that explain reality in strikingly similar ways. There are stories that actually create realities. And there are also stories that explain links between realities. Here are a couple of examples.

NEW ZEALAND AND ROME

I want to include this section, that may not look totally at home with the rest of the subject, because it is a demonstration that myths are significantly universal and human phenomena. The similarities between these two emphasise how human this phenomenon is. New Zealand and Rome have origin myths with amazing similarities. One of them is an oral tradition; the other one is the sequel of an oral poem as recited by a mythical poet (Homer, who narrated *The Iliad*). They both provide links between civilisations.

For the Maori population of New Zealand, it all commences with a tragic love story in Hawaiiki, the original home of the Maori: a group of people leave their land by ship, led by an explorer, Kupe. Their lengthy voyage wandering through a Pacific Ocean full of adventure ends many miles away, when they discover *Aotearoa*, the 'Land of the Long White Cloud'. This is the legend of the discovery of the North Island of New Zealand, orally transmitted by the Maori since they arrived in their new home.

The origin myth of the Latin people commences with the adventures of Aeneas. By making Aeneas, a Trojan, the hero of the *Aeneid*, Virgil takes up the story of one of the characters in Homer's poems, actually providing a palpable link between the Greek and Latin traditions; this is something all Romans were keen to believe (something necessary to validate themselves as a culture, a bit like Christianity used Judaism). The story goes like this: after the war caused by Helen's tragic love story in Troy, and the fall of the city, Aeneas flees and wanders the Mediterranean with a group of followers, until they find a suitable land. They call it *Alba Longa* or *Albalonga*, the 'Land of the Long White Dawn' (*Alba* meaning 'white' and 'dawn' in Latin). They make *Albalonga* their home, until twin brothers called Romulus and Remus are abandoned and suckled by a she-wolf. Romulus eventually founds the city that will become the capital of Latium, Rome, very close to the original site. That is the epic that Virgil wrote as a poem, and that Romans readily adopted as their mythical origin.

As we have seen, myths and realities are closely linked, pretty much like genealogies, real or imagined, connect individuals or societies with their past. The genealogy (and known ethnicity) will definitely influence how the individual thinks of him or herself and may result in different character and personality traits. We will see how the most important myth in history influences Western culture.

THE MYTH OF ADAM & EVE

"... we have to keep on dreaming until we abolish the false boundary between what is illusory and what is tangible, until we achieve our aspirations and discover that the paradise lost was always there, around every corner." – **Julio Cortázar**

There is a way of reading the myth of the Garden of Eden allegorically and thoroughly that makes a lot of sense and and it is not exactly they way Christianity reads it. The way of reading it I mean gives the reader a good idea of how ancient Hebrews saw the world and how that story was told for the first time. One has to begin by assuming that human beings are animals and that they not separate from the rest of creation.

One thing is certain. There was no individual immortal soul when the *Tanakh* was written. Perhaps the clearest indication can be found at the end of the most beautiful and wisest passage of the Ecclesiastes (the one that begins *"To everything there is a season... "*), as it provides unequivocal evidence that the Hebrews understood humans were not separate from other animals and that there was no afterlife: *"I said in my heart concerning the estate of the sonnes of men, that God might manifest them, and that they might see that they themselues are beasts. * For that which befalleth the sonnes of men, befalleth beastes, euen one thing befalleth them: as the one dieth, so dieth the other; yea they haue all one breath, so that a man hath no preheminence aboue a beast; for all is vanitie. All goe vnto one place, all are of the dust, and all turne to dust againe."* [1]

I imagine it is quite clear that where it reads *"they haue all one breath"* the word *'breath'* is not meant literally, but in the ancient Hebrew sense, as in *'being alive' (nephesh)*. And then the verse reinforces the concept with the words *"so that a man hath no preheminence aboue a beast"*.

If there is any doubt about what the author or authors of the Ecclesiastes meant, the two verses that follow the ones above cannot be any clearer: *"Who knoweth the spirit †of man, that † goeth upward; and the spirit of the beast that goeth downeward to the earth? * Wherefore I perceiue that there is nothing better, then that a man should reioyce in his own workes: for that is his portion; for who shall bring him to see what shal be after him?"* [2] That is the Ecclesiastes, III, 21-22. I invite you to check it. Of course many people have read and understand these verses, but there are countless Christians who have no idea that their Bible includes verses like those. Mostly because they have not read it, or because they have not understood it, or because they do not know that the Hebrews believed that rewards and punishments took place here, on Earth, nowhere else. In the Book of Genesis there is more, much more.

Let us have a look at another very prominent example of no punishment in hell: when Moses came down from Mount Sinai, he brought with him the two tablets with the Ten Commandments. On them, among other things, God had ordered: *"20.3.-Thou shalt not make unto thee a graven image, nor any manner of likeness, of any thing that is in heaven above, or that is in the earth beneath, or that is in the water under the earth: 20.4.- thou shalt not bow down unto them, nor serve them; for I the LORD thy God am a jealous God, visiting the iniquity of the fathers upon the children unto the third and fourth generation of them that hate Me"*. Apart from the fact that he mentions other Gods or idols several times —which we shall discuss later— in this particular point He stresses that the punishment would be *"visiting the iniquity of the fathers"* upon the grandchildren and descendants of the sinner. No mention of eternal damnation. No mention of hell. No mention of punishment other than here on Earth.

As we said before, Old Judaism, the Judaism of the Temple, had no concept of individual immortal soul. Ancient religions existed, and their idols and gods existed, to protect the nations and the individuals who believed in them while they were alive. They were basically beliefs that would bring you good luck or protection. You would pray and offer sacrifices in order to obtain a good crop or for your sheep to have more lambs, or not to be attacked by foreign armies. There was no heaven or hell. In general, religions were either idolatrous or polytheistic. Judaism differed from the rest in that it was monotheistic. Its God, Yahweh, had chosen the Jewish tribes as His favourite nation.

Of course, the scribes who compiled the Book of Genesis believed in the God of the Hebrews, so the explanation for the creation of the universe and humanity had to include Him. In the book He has many names: El, Elohim, Adonai, Yahweh. Robert Wright explains this fact in detail in *The evolution of God* (q.v.). It has to do with the development of the notion of the deity of the Jewish nation.

The explanations provided in the Book of Genesis are clear and direct: for instance, why did God create Adam from dust? According to science, life originated billions of years ago from elements not very different from the dust of the ground. The amazing thing is that the explanation of the ancient Hebrews matches exactly the current explanation. They did not have the scientific knowledge we have nowadays, but their explanation was incredibly correct for the time.

Asimov obviously understood the allegory: *"The Biblical writers knew nothing of microscopic life, but dust is not a bad way of describing it, in the absence of knowledge. Microorganisms are as small as dust grains, after all."* [3]

We could say, for instance, that we are mostly made of carbon, hydrogen, nitrogen, calcium, sulphur, sodium, magnesium, etc. Presumably that would satisfy a scientist. It could also be said that we are all made of stardust. It is a poetical way of saying exactly the same thing, as all of those elements can be found in stars, and that is where our whole planet comes from. Even Carl Sagan said at one point that we are star stuff. Well, neither the Hebrews who passed the story from generation to generation, or sang it in tents and around campfires, nor the scribes who compiled the Book of Genesis had access to any of the scientific information Sagan or Asimov had, but they knew we were made of dust. That was the first myth that had to do with human beings: what our body is made of. Is there any better way to explain the composition of the human body to illiterate shepherds?

The allegory is not that God was a potter, or that He was a magician. According to the allegory, God made human beings out of dust because that is what human beings are made of. The *Torah* could have said that God made Adam *ex nihilo*, from nothing, because He could have done that. But the allegory says He made him from dust. And the reason is very clear. The authors knew that the human body is made of tiny particles and that, after death, it returns to being tiny particles. But let's go back to the Garden of Eden.

Also, I have to clarify here that there are many detailed theories as to who wrote the Book of Genesis, and the Bible in general, and many in-depth studies that have analysed the type of writing, the events described, the language, the names of the people, the toponymy (for example, Mount Sinai is sometimes called Mount Horeb), the Greek translated words (whether they were taken from Hebrew or Aramaic or other source languages), etc. On those bases, it has been determined that there are four or five or even more individuals — including P (Priestly) and J (Yahwist), E (Elohist), D (Deuteronomist) and even Ezra, the prophet— who were the actual co-authors, collators, or editors of the Old Testament, and probably about as many others who wrote the New Testament. Determining who wrote what is the work of Bible historians and theologians. Speculations as to whether this passage or that passage was written in the late Persian or the Hellenistic period, or whether "P" or "J" or "D" were the authors of a passage lie beyond the scope of this book. The point of this chapter is to explore new ideas about the Bible and link them to Christianity and the West, to answer some questions and maybe to leave the door open for some more questions to be asked.

But let us go back to interpreting the allegory, let us turn this whole thing around and see it from another, much more rational, perspective. Let us apply critical thinking to understand the allegory and simplify the situation. If we read the Book of Genesis again we might find that this is a story about two individuals of the *Homo Sapiens* species from the Hebrew perspective at the time it was written, when they knew they were part of the animal kingdom. Yes, the first human beings. Arguably, the Hebrews didn't know anything about the taxonomy of the genera, of the species, or of the *Homo Erectus* species —comparatively, that is a very recent concept— but they had not forgotten that they were animals. They also guessed that at one point or another humans had acquired a high degree of consciousness (what Christians called *soul* and Greeks called *psyche*).

We know that when a new species is created, an old species splits into two. We know that at one point, individuals of the genus *Homo* became what we now call *Homo Sapiens.*

Then— and this is extremely important and logical—let us say that, in the Hebrew myth, Adam and Eve were not meant to be the only individuals of the genus *Homo*. Let us say that the Book of Genesis describes the moment when Adam and Eve, a male and a female of the genus *Homo*, or the *Homo Erectus* species <u>became</u> *Homo Sapiens*. The point in time when they evolved. The point when they became a separate species. That would be fairly acceptable to a scientist. They did not look white, blond and hairless like the ones in the European version of the Garden of Eden we were taught at school (perhaps we should imagine them as any of the primates that are part of our real ancestry).

Let us call them hominins. I am not sure if this is very scientific, but it will serve our purposes.

The poetry of the myth is that they ate from the Tree of the Knowledge of Good and Evil. That obviously means that at that point they acquired reason. They acquired a soul if you like. They became conscious. In so doing, they were indeed the first and only human beings, but they were not the only hominins on the planet. There is a lot of evidence of what the Hebrew myth means. What the *Torah* describes is what happened in Eden when two of these hominins became human. It is the incredible moment when our ancestors became self-aware. *"Their eyes were opened"*. The awakening of human consciousness. The ancient myth transcribed in the *Torah* attempts to find the point in the continuum of evolution in which our ancestors became human. If we think of it that way, the whole thing makes sense. The *Torah* does not mention *psyche* not because the Hebrews had not considered the concept of the human mind, of human awareness, but because they thought that being alive (*nephesh*) was the most important gift from *Yahweh*. But obviously, having Genesis introduced the concept of the difference between good and evil gives us an idea that they were considering a qualitative and progressive difference between animal mind and human mind. Greeks began talking about *psyche* at a much later stage. It is evident that, for the Hebrews, human beings were part of the animal kingdom. Humans were animals. Special animals that could think, communicate and even write, but the most important concept for them at that stage was their *nephesh*. They were alive. The Hebrews understood that humanity, though, had to have started at some point and that the change had brought consequences.

And this is the part of the allegory most people interested in the subject (both creationists and evolutionists alike) seem to misunderstand. Some may equate the Tree of the Knowledge of Good and Evil with consciousness, but their interpretation is that Adam and Eve were human from the moment they were created and that there was nobody else like them on the face of the Earth. If we literally believe what St Paul and St Augustine wanted to believe —that they were the only ones of the species on Earth— then the Book of Genesis becomes utter nonsense. The only logical interpretation is that they were two hominins among many who roamed Africa or the Middle East, in clans, family groups or as couples. The only difference is that at one point those two primates had to become human for the human species to exist. The Book of Genesis says our species commenced when our ancestors started reasoning and became aware of their own existence. It is quite evident that ancient Hebrews had been transmitting, from time immemorial, the myth that described the evolutionary process as we now know it happened.

I would say that the scribes who wrote Genesis transcribed, fixing in writing, a series of traditional Semitic stories that perceived the evolution of the human species in a much more Darwinian fashion than we all tend to assume nowadays, after centuries of anthropocentric delusions of grandeur.

Not that the result of that was a bad one. Having misunderstood this book of unequalled historical significance was a mistake, but that mistake gave Christianity and the West an extremely positive view of ourselves and of our individuality. The consequences of which are evident in the progress of the West.

What the ancient Hebrews knew and science is just beginning to comprehend is that Adam (our first ancestor, not the one in the Bible or the myth), was an ape who did not look like a modern human at all.

I now quote from an article from Pickrell Lab online that discusses the discovery that the Y-chromosome that links all males to one common ancestor is much older than previously thought: *"The implicit assumption here (the reason Elhaik et al. find the numbers 'extraordinarily early' and 'astonishing') is that the individual carrying the most recent common ancestor of all human Y chromosomes (AKA 'Adam') should be an anatomically modern human... From the point of view of population genetics, there is absolutely no reason that the common ancestor of all human Y chromosomes must have existed in an individual that we would identify as 'human'."*

Why is it important to come to this conclusion? Because it logically and unequivocally points to the fact that the most consequential book humanity ever conceived —whether we believe in God or not— has been grossly misinterpreted by Christianity (and Islam) for many, many generations. In Christianity this equivocation ended up fostering individuality. The Hebrew myth provided a lyrical, magical, explanation of our own evolution.

Descartes, with seventeenth-century sophistication, came up with the concept of self-awareness as a *sine qua non* for humanity: *"Cogito ergo sum"*, he stated. "I think therefore I am". We know we exist. We are human. That is our expulsion from the Garden of Eden. But the authors of the *Torah* did not imagine any sin. The sin came with St Paul's delirious interpretation... and with St Augustine's obsession with sex, as we shall see.

The *Torah* says that God created human beings after all the other animals. We know human beings appeared after other animals. In our current stage of evolution we are fairly recent. According to the tradition of the Hebrews, Adam and Eve had become, in a way, closer to God. That is the meaning of *"In his own image and likeness"*. Not because humans look like God or God looks like a man. The myth goes on to say that rather than a blessing awareness became something akin to a curse. Because of that loss of innocence, they would behave differently from all other animals. They would need to work and keep on improving their lot. And they would suffer in ways that are unique to the species.

"In the sweate of thy face shall thou eate bread, till thou returne vnto the ground: for out of it wast thou taken, for dust thou art, and vnto dust shalt thou returne". [4] Men would need to eventually learn to use the fire with which to bake the bread and cook their food. They would need to plant the wheat, harvest it and grind it and bake it. They would need to make clothes (as only humans do), build dwellings, and look after their families. And then they would die and become dust again.

Humanity faced a future of work and finitude. And there was no going back. In Genesis, the angels with their swords were keeping these two primates away from the world of the other animals. Not as a punishment, but because there was no way they could go back. What had been lost was Paradise, immanent in the primal innocence of the animal.

After speaking to Adam, God turned to Eve: *"Unto the woman he said, I will greatly multiply thy sorowe and thy conception. In sorow thou shalt bring forth children..."* [5] Childbirth in humans is much more traumatic and painful than it is for other animals. Humans have larger brains that require a larger cranium.

Walking upright has made the pelvis and birth canal develop in such a way that it means that the baby has to turn on its way out. Birth in other animals is less traumatic. And the females of other species don't cry in pain as women do. Maybe that has to do with not wanting to call the attention of predators at a time when they are very vulnerable.

The Book of Genesis appears to say that language and humanity were almost simultaneous. In fact, the more we look at them the more they appear to be one and the same. Even if we try not to philosophise about this point, we can safely say that language, inasmuch as it is fundamental for the creation of thought processes, is absolutely essential for humanity to exist, for anyone to be part of the *Homo Sapiens* species. Eve spoke to Adam. Adam followed Eve's advice to eat. They spoke and they knew. They were not literally eating. Of course there was no tree of the knowledge of good and evil. They were communicating an idea and in doing so they became aware. They became human.

AWARENESS OF MORTALITY

Maybe it would be better to interpret —as the Hebrews probably did— that Yahweh *warned* Adam and Eve not to eat from the Tree of the Knowledge of Good and Evil, because, if they did there would be consequences (*"or you will surely die"*). Whey would He have ordered them not to eat? Christians have no explanation for the attitude.

I believe the translator from Hebrew or Aramaic to Greek perhaps could not catch the subtlety of the original term. Maybe in Hebrew the word was closer to "warn", which has connotations that are very different to those of "order". God was warning these two apes not to eat, the same way a mother or a father tells a toddler not to touch the fire, because if they do, there will be consequences: the most important of which will be pain. In this case, consciousness and knowledge carried consequences. Some were bad and some were good.

So Yahweh did not *threaten* them with death. He warned them. Yes, death became real only because they were conscious of it.

Primates and other animals may have a degree of self-awareness, but only human beings comprehend that they are going to eventually die. And 'eventually' is the operative word here, as humans are aware of their mortality not because they may be in danger, but because they know that in the long run their fate is death. So, according to the *Torah*, God kept His promise. Hobbes's evaluation of the situation is close to our reading. He states in the *Leviathan*: *"Not that actual death then entered; for Adam then could never have had children; whereas he lived long after, and saw a numerous posterity ere he died. But where it is said, (Gen.ii.17) In the day that thou eatest thereof, thou shalt surely die, it must needs be meant of his mortality, and certitude of death."* [1] Of course, it means 'certitude of death'. As an ape, he did not know he was going to die. As a thinking *Homo Sapiens* he became certain of his eventual death.

THE MYSTERY OF CAIN'S WIFE

Adam and Eve had two sons. Cain was one of them and Abel was the other. Cain killed his brother Abel and, after that, he was sent to wander the earth in punishment. Cain was afraid and begged God not to banish him "... whoever finds me will kill me". Who would kill him if there was no human on Earth other than his parents? Christianity has no explanation for that.

Asimov desperately tries to find an explanation: *"Who is the 'every-one'? ... the total population of Earth at the time of the murder of Abel was three: Adam, Eve, and Cain. Could it be that Adam and Eve had many children, who have gone unnamed and unmentioned but now populate the world? ... Could it be that the Creation-myths of the P-document and the J-document refer to two different sets of the works of God? Perhaps God created human beings, male and female, many of them on the sixth day of Creation, and they filled the Earth. Afterward, it may be, he created Adam and Eve, alone in the Garden, as the progenitors of a particular family.*

Thus Cain would now fear death at the hands of any of the numerous 'pre-Adamites'." He was very close.

Eventually Cain reappears in the picture, this time with a wife. So, then? Christianity has no explanation for the existence of the wife.

Greenblatt describes the doubts a young man called La Peyrère (another one obsessed by the Bible and the questions with no answer to them) might have had and how he tried to solve the puzzle: *"And what was the woman Cain married doing in the land of Nod? And how could the fugitive have built a city there, without any other people around to inhabit it? Might all of these clues suggest, the boy asked himself, that there were already humans in the world before the creation of Adam and Eve, humans who lived outside the walls of the Garden of Eden and with whom Adam and Eve and their offspring interacted?"* [1]

Asimov asks himself the question and comes back with the same answer: *"Another possibility is the one mentioned in connection with Cain's fear of being killed as an outlaw that numerous pre-Adamites existed and that Cain married one of those."* [2].

As we said, they were very close. But they always thought in terms of human beings, not hominins. Logically, La Peyrère thought in Rabbinical/Christian terms, not in Darwinian terms, as in those days that would have been counter-intuitive. Asimov thought in terms of pre-Adamites and not that Adam was one among many. Maybe he thought of apes, but did not explain the difference between primates and pre-Adamites. He gives the impression that they are human beings.

The way I read it, and the way I believe was imagined by the ancient Hebrews when they wrote the myth was that the wife must have been a female primate from another group. Otherwise, how can you explain her existence? Before then, his words *"whoever finds me..."* could not have referred to any animals other than hominins. The only logical interpretation is that the Book of Genesis depicts the beginning of consciousness among hominins.

HOW HUMANITY SPREAD AMONG THE HOMININS

*A*nother part of the Book of Genesis that has been the object of several farfetched interpretations is VI: 1-4): *"And it came to passe, when men began to multiply on the face of the earth, and daughters were borne vnto them, that the sonnes of God saw the daughters of men that they were faire and they took them wiues of all which they chose. And the Lord said, my spirit shall not alwayes striue with man, for that hee also is flesh: yet his dayes shalbe an hundred and twenty yeeres. There were Giants in the earth in those daies; and also after that, when the sonnes of God came in vnto the daughters of men, and they bare children to them, the same became mighty men which were of old, men of renowne."* [1]

The word *"giants"* is obviously an infelicity of the translation. What was meant was *"great men"*, or *"mighty men"*, as they are described towards the end. The descendants of Adam and Eve would have been more intelligent and better skilled than those without the seeds of language and culture, with a lower degree of consciousness, and would have probably become leaders of other hominins. Indeed, those sons of God would have been individuals who were already human, otherwise why include that quotation from God between two references to godlike men (*sons of God*) (*"And the Lord said, My spirit shall not always strive with man, for that he <u>also</u> is flesh: yet his days shall be an hundred and twenty years"*)? [My italics]. What God says would tally with the rest of the allegory in the Garden of Eden. Human beings are animals like the rest of the apes. Is God saying that men have a soul but that their soul would only last while they are alive, i.e., one hundred and twenty years? Ah… the words *psyche* or consciousness would have been so useful at the time!

The way language spread among humans was reproduced in an experiment with chimpanzees. In 1967, Allen and Beatrix Gardner, two American anthropologists, taught Washoe, a female chimpanzee, how to speak Ameslan, the American sign language. She was the first non human who could communicate using a language. She taught sign language to her adopted child, and later on, when she was introduced to other chimpanzees, they all learnt Ameslan as well. Washoe demonstrated that she had some degree of self-awareness and emotion.

Asimov cannot find an explanation in terms of what the Bible says about the *"sons of God"*: he does not even try resorting to his "pre-Adamites": *"If the sons of God were divine and enforced their will on helpless human women, why would Earth have to suffer for that?"*. [2]

Wright finds that this passage is an exception in the normally monotheistic Hebrew Bible: *"Though much of the scripture assumes the existence of only one God, some parts strike a different tone. The book of Genesis recalls the time when a bunch of male deities came down and had sex with attractive human females; these* gods *'went in to the daughters of humans, who bore children to them.'* (*And not ordinary children: 'These were the heroes that were of old, warriors of renown')*"³

My reading is that two very important things are being said here: the first one is that males of the *Sapiens* species mated with females of other less advanced *Homo* species, as they were still attractive to them, even after the split between the species (after the separation, there is a period when individuals of one species are still attracted to the other species; we now know about interspecies miscegenation with Neanderthals and Denisovans at least). The second one is confirmation in this paragraph that Hebrews knew that human beings were animals, and that the soul in them dies when their body dies, like the rest of the animals: "*My spirit shall not always strive with man, for that he <u>also</u> is flesh*". Human beings may be conscious, but they are still animals.

Propagation might have happened in several places at the same time, although science and Genesis agree on a monogenetic origin in terms of the first human beings, i.e., Adam and Eve. Then Genesis speaks very clearly of propagation: Cain goes out to look for a wife. In terms of the myth of creation and, for an explanation provided by people of the 8th century BC, the *Torah* illustrates the propagation of our species amazingly well. The use of consciousness and language appear to have spread fairly rapidly: Cain and his wife had male children who needed females to procreate. The phenomenon probably repeated itself with less advanced *Sapiens* females, but also with *Neanderthal*, and maybe *Denisovan* ones; that's what Genesis refers to.

What science knows now with some certainty is that *Neanderthal* females and *Sapiens* males met and began to mate approximately 370,000 years ago.

Neanderthal and *Sapiens* "Y" chromosomes are more similar between each other than with respect to those of *Denisovans*. It is possible that the *Denisovans* had been so much farther East that they never met any *Sapiens*.

What has been proved is that *Neanderthals* and *Sapiens* have a shared history. In terms of evolution the result was that the "Y" chromosome of the *Neanderthals* slowly disappeared and that the *Sapiens* one ended up totally replacing it.

Regarding what Genesis says, Asimov cannot find a right answer to the riddle: *"If the interpretation of the first part of the verse is God's self-reminder that man is mortal, then the remainder of the verse is a punishment for human corruption. The mortality of man is emphasized."* [4] He reads it like St Paul would have read it.

This is one of the instances in which the *Torah* uses the phrase "sons of God" referring to *Sapiens* individuals. Much later, Jesus of Nazareth would be quoted using that phrase to refer to himself. Aslan doubts the authenticity of the quote: *"Nor, by the way, did Jesus call himself 'Son of God,' another title that others seem to have ascribed to him."* [5] The title was sometimes used to refer to Jewish kings.

Genesis uses a language that only interpreted in the correct way makes any sense at all: *"And it came to pass, when men began to multiply on the face of the earth, and daughters were borne vnto them, that the sonnes of God saw the daughters of men that they were faire and they took them wiues of all which they chose..."*. In the context of the development of humanity according to the explanation of the *Tanach*, "*sons of God*" cannot be interpreted as "*deities*". The only possibility is that some human beings were more advanced than others. After the Myth of Eden and Adam and Eve, there were human beings who had consciousness.

On the other hand, the claim that Jesus used the phrase "son of God" to refer to himself maybe was misinterpreted or misconstrued in Nicaea to convince the bishops that Jesus was God. It worked.

CHRISTIAN INTERPRETATION OF THE BOOK OF GENESIS

$\mathcal{L}$et us start by imagining we agree with a literal or semi-literal interpretation of the Book of Genesis, what most Christians believe about it (and let us try to make it sound as logical as possible): God created Adam from dust. Then He created Eve from his rib. They were the first human beings. He put them in the Garden of Eden. He ordered them not to eat from a tree. He said if they did they would surely die. Then the Devil, disguised as a snake, tempted Eve and convinced her that she should eat from the tree. Eve disobeyed God and persuaded Adam to do that as well. They both ate an apple. They discovered they were naked and they probably had sex, although that is not quite clear. God, in a fit of rage (?), expelled them from the Garden of Eden. He told Adam that he would have to work and that he would die and turn to dust. He told Eve she would hate snakes and would give birth with pain... But then, after they ate the apple, they did not die, even when God had said they would. He was wrong. God was wrong? Later they had two sons, Cain and Abel. Cain killed Abel. God became very angry (again?) with him and sent him away. He went away but was scared that somebody would kill him. Who, if there was nobody else on Earth? Literally. He came back with a wife. Who, if there was nobody else on Earth? ...and so on and so forth. The Christian interpretation that Adam and Eve were the only human beings on the planet does not appear to make sense. It does not make any sense at all. No part of it does. And there are no Christian explanations for any of that.

Was the snake the Devil? There is no Devil in the *Torah*. In Judaism the Devil is only an obstacle in our path to do good. It is not a fallen angel or a demon. The snake is only an allegory for an obstacle. Then the Devil, a subsequent Christian concept, a Christian adaptation to the Myth, only makes sense when Christianity adds the idea of "sin".

The way Christianity explains what St Paul interpreted from the Myth doesn't make that much sense either. <u>According to him, Adam and Eve had been created immortal.</u> That is what he proposed. We don't know if he meant it literally. Because of their sin, God told them they would die, and then they became mortal. That punishment was extended to all of their descendants for ever more. That's why we are now mortal. But that cannot be a punishment. Knowing that we are going to die is part of having consciousness. St Paul, however, was introducing the concept of the human immortal soul. Something that survives. A new concept.

The Bishop of Lyon from 189 BC, Ireneus, named the sin committed in the Garden of Eden: he called it Original Sin. We still don't know what the Original Sin is all about. St Augustin proposed it was concupiscence (sexual desire). His theory was accepted for a long time. Many religious communities still believe that's what it is. The thing is, if Adam and

Eve had sex, why would that be a sin if God had ordered them to go forth and multiply? Also, if they had not had sex, we would not be here to talk about it.

What made it even more interesting in terms of the explanation of Paradise given by St Paul was the inclusion of Jesus Christ in the picture, in a Hebrew myth that predated Jesus by many centuries. Adam and Eve had committed a 'crime' that all of humanity would have to pay for ever and ever, having to be mortal when we could have lived eternally. However, through baptism and belief in Jesus, Christians gain immortality again, this time the immortality of the soul. The whole structure seems fairly weak and not very rational. Obviously, not what the Hebrews had wanted to say with their allegory. Yes... that means the immortal soul. Something that had not been considered before. The way it was introduced in the Myth of Eden does not make a lot of sense. It doesn't matter. The transcendence of the individual immortal soul was worth the trouble. If Paul was going to base his religion on Judaism and he had to link both religions, the immortal soul had to begin at some point, and the best point was at the beginning. As I was saying, it does not make much sense, but that was a price he was willing to pay, I imagine. Christianity needed the immortal soul. It needed the attraction to create a universal religion. In summary, St Paul introduced the idea that Adam and Eve had been created immortal (!) and that, through their original sin, they had lost that immortality. The loss extended to their descendants (the whole of the human species). Only through Jesus' intercession—he said—the immortality of the soul is regained. St Paul's quirky interpretation of Genesis had a desired effect: it established the individual immortal soul as a fact.

Europeans and Christians of all backgrounds believed that notion for many centuries. It also had long-term unexpected consequences: it gave humans not only a superior status but it set them apart from other animals.

My reading is that the individual immortal soul actually separated them from the rest of nature as well— which was somehow necessary to allow 'objective' observation— and because of that, it arguably resulted in the development of science and technology, the industrial revolution, and eventually capitalism. Farfetched? Well, individuality is a unique Western trait and the West is Christian. That is not a coincidence. It was something essential for the development of Western institutions.

Stephen Greenblatt believes the Garden of Eden is central to the way we have developed: *"Whether we believe in the story of Adam and Eve or regard it as an absurd fiction, we have been made in its image. Over many centuries, the story has shaped the way we think about crime and punishment, moral responsibility, death, pain, work, leisure, companionship, marriage, gender, curiosity, sexuality, and our shared humanness. Had history developed in a different direction, the Enuma Elish, the Atrahasis, and the epic of Gilgamesh might have served as our own bundle of origin stories and would undoubtedly have shaped us other than as we are. That it did not work out this way had consequences."* [1] I could not agree more.

And what does Christianity mention about disobedience? Well, as we said before, the Christian interpretation explains that there is an order that is disobeyed, not a warning. That's why there is a punishment.

Talking about *Paradise lost*, by Milton, Harold Bloom says: *"Many years ago I wrote a commentary on the Yahwist strand in the Torah and remember saying that the misfortune of Eve and of Adam is akin to remarking: 'When we were children, we were terribly punished for being children'. Milton would not have cared for that' Blake and Shelley might have approved. Why should we accept the word 'foul' for the mischance of our first parents?"* [2]

Why did God tell Adam he would have to work as a punishment if work is a good thing? Well, in Eden he didn't have to work and now he would have to start. That does not mean that work is something bad. That wouldn't have made any sense at all. Many things had changed in the Hebrew myth but there was no punishment. That would not have made any sense. Why would Eve have to have children with pain? Was that a punishment? Again, before it made sense, but not after St Paul. Childbirth cannot be a punishment because that's what women have to do for humanity to go forth and multiply, which is part of the original message from God. Why did they cover themselves? Why were they embarrassed to be naked? Wearing clothes is something very human, although not all human beings wear clothes. It has to do with self-awareness, I suppose, nothing else. The had acquired consciousness, and with that, modesty.

Well, we have seen answers to some of those questions. Let us try to find some more in a systematic way. We will see that some questions are answered by applying common sense and some other questions answer themselves.

It is evident, for all to see, that Paul and the Christian theologians that followed him introduced notions that were totally alien to the *Torah*; notions like the original physical immortality of humans, the individual immortal soul, original sin, afterlife, heaven, hell, the devil, eternity, etc. None of those ideas had anything to do with the world of the Hebrews. The allegory was misinterpreted (or, I would say, intentionally embellished by St Paul). What is extraordinary is that that misinterpretation had the consequences it had. It definitely gave a new direction to the Roman understanding of the universe and resulted in Western civilisation. The human individual that St Paul introduced was almost divine. Any human individual.

The way St Paul and his followers interpreted the Book of Genesis was, of course, influenced by his new ideas after converting to Christianity, or 'creating' Christianity, if you like. But when you change a concept as radically and thoroughly as they did, things tend not to add up somewhere. The doctrine was there, and doctrines are there to be believed. The Book of Genesis, as understood by the Fathers of the Church would not accept an exegesis. Whoever attempted one would be committing a mortal sin. That is a very clever way of hiding any incoherence the dogma has: we don't talk about it.

Christopher Hitchens believed, along with many of his creationist foes, that Scripture and the theory of evolution (Darwin) were mutually exclusive. Well, it's not quite like that. Also, believing in God does not necessarily imply believing in an immortal soul. Or in any of the fabrications introduced by organised Christianity. As we said, the ancient Hebrews did not believe in an immortal soul. Contrary to Christopher Hitchens' opinion, people do not believe in God just because they are afraid of dying.

As I write this, *The American Catholic* quotes Pope Francis saying *"And I believe in God, not in a Catholic God, there is no Catholic God..."*. That appears to be a sign that doctrinal religion will slowly turn towards a deist God , like the God of the Enlightenment. Maybe I'm giving it a meaning it doesn't have.

Greenblatt wonders about the reasons for the pervasiveness of the literal reading of Genesis: *"An insistence on the story's literal truth, an actual Adam and Eve in an actual garden became one of the cornerstones of Christian orthodoxy. This insistence lies at the center of my own fascination with the story of Adam and Eve. How does something made-up become so compellingly real? How does a stone statue begin to breathe or a wooden puppet learn to stand up on its own and to dance without strings? And what happens when fictional creatures behave as if they were alive? Are they fated for that reason to begin to die?"* [3]

Well, if we have to talk about real reality, and here the redundancy applies, there are no trees of the knowledge of good and evil, and if there were, they would not produce apples (or figs, as in the Tanach). There never were any speaking serpents, and if there were, they would not have been the Devil, because the Devil, as conceived by Christians, did not exist in the 8th century BC, which is when that part of the Book of Genesis became Scripture. Christianity *had* to invent in order to exist.

What interests us for this analysis is the difference between the original meaning of the *Tanakh* (the Jewish Bible) and the Christian version decreed by St Paul and followed by all Christian denominations. Rabbinic Judaism appears to have kept pretty much to the view of their ancestors. Mohammed followed the Christian view of Genesis blindly without having understood the allegory either.

As we have repeated, time and time again, in Rabbinical Judaism there is no heaven or hell, no afterlife. That should not surprise anyone. It is logical, as ancient Judaism, the religion of the Temple, did not have a heaven or a hell either. The Hebrews did not believe in an afterlife, nor did they believe in an individual immortal soul. If you were a good person, your reward was here. If you were bad, your punishment was here too. The word "*nephesh*", used 750 times in the 24 books of the *Tanakh*, or Hebrew Bible (including the *Torah*), which many Christians understand as '*soul*', means '*breath of life*' —as we saw before—, but has nothing to do with individuals and it has nothing to do with 'consciousness'. You could use the word to mean '*life*' in all humans or animals, or maybe plants as well. The words '*neshamah*' and '*ruah*' were also used to mean something akin to 'soul', but not exactly what was understood by Christian 'soul'. In all cases, the word used to mean 'soul' in the *Torah* is connected to the body and its material needs and wants. It has nothing to do with immortality or the afterlife.

Isaac Asimov provides an explanation very similar to mine: "*Nowadays, a common view of the soul is that it is some sort of spiritual essence, utterly immaterial, that is inserted into a person at birth (or at conception) and that departs from a person at death; that it is an immortal component of man that is neither born nor dies but is housed in the body for the brief period of that body's existence on Earth. All this is actually derived from Greek thought, and in that sense, "soul" is a translation of the Greek psyche and not of the Hebrew nephesh.*" [4] Similar to what I understand, but not quite the same. I believe Aristotle had come close to the notion of the immortal soul but was not totally convinced. The way I see it, some Greeks philosophers (Socrates and Plato in particular) had the idea and St Paul refined it. Whether that was right or wrong, that is a different matter.

Why is Genesis important? Well, the Book of Genesis is the most widely read among the different versions of the origins of humanity, especially in the West. But it has one added advantage over any other version: the Book of Genesis —just like the Rosetta Stone that provided three linguistic versions of one text and enabled Champollion to decipher hieroglyphs and opened up the Egyptian cosmology— was written by the ancient Hebrews and has had different interpretations at different times; it has been interpreted by Christians, Rabbinic Jews and Muslims. Three different cosmovisions.

What happens is that the Book of Genesis was taken from an ancient Semitic myth that had to be interpreted allegorically, but allegorically from a Hebrew perspective. The Christian interpretation had some literally incredible twists of its own.

God created human beings and then he ordered them not to eat from a tree lest they die, and then he forbade them to eat from another tree (the tree of life) or they would live forever. Christopher Hitchens believed that this was absurd and contradictory. And he was an intelligent and well-read man. Taken literally, it is indeed absurd and contradictory.

Somebody else who took the story literally, lock, stock and barrel, is Richard Dawkins:

"Original Sin itself comes straight from the Old Testament myth of Adam and Eve. Their sin – eating the fruit of a forbidden tree – seems mild enough to merit a mere reprimand. But the symbolic nature of the fruit (knowledge of good and evil, which in practice turned out to be knowledge that they were naked) was enough to turn their scrumping escapade into the mother and father of all sins.* They and all their descendants were banished forever from the Garden of Eden, deprived of the gift of eternal life, and condemned to generations of painful labour, in the field and in childbirth respectively." [5]

The asterisk in the quotation is a footnote that proves, even more convincingly, that Dawkins' interpretation is unbelievably literal. I reproduce the footnote as well:

"* I am aware that 'scrumping' will not be familiar to American readers. But I enjoy reading unfamiliar American words and looking them up to broaden my vocabulary. I have deliberately used a few other region-specific words for this reason. Scrumping itself is a mot juste of unusual economy. It doesn't just mean stealing: it specifically means stealing apples and only apples. It is hard for a mot to get more juste than that. Admittedly the Genesis story doesn't specify that the fruit was an apple, but tradition has long held it so." [6]

The original sin, the punishment, the disobedience and the transgression that required the atonement of the human species forever, were the result of some imaginative individuals, beginning with St Paul and including St Augustine and St Jerome.

As with many other Christian interpretations of the *Torah*, this one had far-reaching consequences. It resulted in widespread misogyny that lasted several centuries. Eve was guilty of everything (even though she had not been created when God issued the warning). Greenblatt explains: *"This endless harping on Eve's sin and the defects or all of her daughters obviously suited the mental world of monks and friars who had taken vows of chastity and abjured –at least officially– the companionship of the other sex. And it suited as well those husbands who were locked in a struggle to dominate their wives and daughters. The miseries brought by Eve became a standard talking point in the battle of the sexes, a predictable and highly useful charge because it seemed to carry the authority of the Bible itself".* [7]

HUMANS AS PRIMATES

*P*eople often acknowledge Lucretius, the first century BC Roman poet, as one of the forerunners of evolutionism. In his epic poem *De rerum natura (The way things are)* he stated, among other things, that the world had not been created by a god. The universe, he said, was the product of a sequence of events. And he did anticipate modern evolutionary theory to some extent. He exerted a massive influence on European evolutionary thinkers from the seventeenth century onwards.

Lucretius depicted the sad, difficult life of our primitive ancestors:

"Of sun withdrawn forever. But their care

Was rather that the clans of savage beasts

Would often make their sleep-time horrible

For those poor wretches; and, from home y-driven,

They'd flee their rocky shelters at approach

Of boar, the spumy-lipped, or lion strong,

And in the midnight yield with terror up

To those fierce guests their beds of out-spread leaves." [1]

Lucretius did not refer to our human ancestors as apes, but he did make it quite clear that they were not much better than animals. And he did reject the existence of an immortal soul. It would seem the idea of an individual immortal soul was an object of debate at the time.

We have seen that a few centuries earlier Aristotle, by using the word *zoon* when referring to human beings, appears to have implied that human beings were apes. No doubt, that was the natural understanding in the days of the *Torah* and before, when all the biblical stories originated: humans were considered apes. We were descended from animals.

Did the Hebrews understand this during Hezekiah's time, when at least part of the Bible was compiled? Or had the traditions and stories already lost their original meaning? If we put the question into chronological perspective, Aristotle lived in the 4th century BC and Hezekiah in the 8th century BC. Even allowing for the fact that they were located in two different geographic areas, the fact that there was a gap of four centuries between the two, and that Aristotle still considered himself a primate gives me a clear indication that people in Hezekiah's time were still aware of our animal origins, i.e., pretty much proto-Darwinian in their ideas.

Even though Judah was becoming slowly urbanised, they probably understood those traditions and legends in their original meaning. We have to remember that this was the early Iron Age and that living in caves, for instance, was not strange.

THE MYTH OF ADAM AND EVE AND THE ENDU... 53

The majority of human beings were not city dwellers, even in the days of Jesus Christ. Many, like John the Baptist and his mother, or before then, Lot and his daughters, lived in caves in the desert. And of course, for many generations, Hebrews lived in tents like the Bedouin nowadays.

There are stories in the Bible that may allegorically refer to different stages of human evolution. Isaac, for instance, was tricked into giving his inheritance to Jacob, his youngest son. Isaac was blind and Jacob made him believe he was Esau, the eldest, by covering his hands with goatskin. Apparently, Esau, a hunter, was extremely hirsute. When Isaac touched Jacob's hands, he thought Jacob was Esau. The strange part of this old story is that Esau was so hirsute that his hands felt like the skins of goats. Allegory or exaggeration? The story refers to the period of the early settlement of Canaan. It has several readings, both literal and allegorical. In the days of Abraham and Isaac, towns were not the norm in Canaan, many people still lived in the open, in caves, or were nomads. The question is: When the Bible was written, did they think that all humans had always been totally developed? Or perhaps that there were some humans that were less developed than others? Maybe the story makes reference to the Edomites, Esau's descendants, who lived in current day Jordan, where Petra is. The *Torah* does not regard them as very advanced. The thing is: if it was reasonable to think that a human could be as hairy as a goat, the mental gap between human and animal was not as wide as it was to become later.

Stephanie Moser, an iconography specialist, attempts an explanation:

"Another biblical figure who conveyed a sense of the distant past was Esau, the brother of Jacob. Esau is described as being hairy all over

and is frequently depicted as a wildman. The description of his physical appearance as hairy relates to his status as a hunter who lived in the wild. It also relates to his being the forefather of the Edomite nation, who may have been perceived by the Hebrews as hunters."[2] What Moser does not explain quite well is why hunters were supposed to be hirsute. Was there the impression that there were humans who were at different stages of evolution? The Hebrews, of course, did not understand concepts like genus and species. Maybe I am reading too much here, but it is possible.

As I state above, nowadays we know that in Europe, tens of thousands of years ago, Cro-Magnon individuals coexisted and interbred with Neanderthals. There were other, closely related, apes that coexisted with humans and were less advanced, like the Denisovans. Is it possible that in the Middle East the knowledge of those species had survived until biblical times? Again, it is possible.

Moser confirms that at a later stage, in classical times, barbarians were depicted as primitive, i.e., that outsiders or enemies were vilified that way:

"It was thus, at this early stage, that key icons for signifying the distant past were established, including the club, the animal skin, nakedness, hairiness and dark skin colour. These attributes effectively became visual symbols that played a critical role in communicating primitiveness and in separating non-Greeks and non-Romans. They signified an outsider or barbarian status and summed up the qualities of the non civilized existence."[3]

So, even when this did not depict Romans or Greeks, there was an idea that there were humans who might not have been as evolved as others. Through St Paul, Christians may have inherited the concept, but understood it as a difference between Christians and pagans. Moser explains:

"In a general sense the visual icons developed in early Christian, medieval and Renaissance times functioned as part of a wider dialogue on how non-Christians were to be defined. This dialogue was inherently visual and relied on symbolic ways of conveying the primitiveness of a pagan existence." [4]

Early Christians obviously never gave a second thought to the fact that, if there were human beings who were not very advanced or not very civilised in the Bible, it was possible that the ancestors of the whole of humanity were not very advanced or very civilised either. My conclusion is that, *a contrario sensu*, it is very possible that ancient Hebrews had the intuition that humans were apes.

THE IMMORTAL SOUL

"... because that sky so blue that we all see is neither heaven nor is it blue. Such a pity that all that beauty is not true!" – **Lupercio Leonardo de Argensola**

In ancient times, people asked themselves whether the soul humans had was different from the rest of the other animals because they knew we were aware; they knew we had consciousness. Well, we do. We have consciousness. We have reached a level of consciousness that is unequalled among animals and, as far as we know, unequalled in the universe. Is it really unequalled in the universe? That is what we believe. We have not found anything similar. Scientists would say that we will have the answer when we find out whether it is the probable result of natural selection or if it is an incredible stroke of luck. Probable events occur frequently. Improbable events rarely do. Until now we have not found vestiges of intelligent life anywhere else in the universe.

The other question Greek philosophers asked —as we saw before— was: *"Are our souls immortal"*? Some believed they were. St Paul and the Fathers of the Church answered with a resounding "Yes".

The debate among theologians and philosophers over the immortality of the soul lasted for centuries. St Paul revived it successfully after the death of Jesus.

Plato, in his dialogue with Glaucon, in the Republic, was very enthusiastic about the immortality of the soul: *"But if you will listen to me, and believe that the soul is immortal and able to endure all evil and all good, we shall always hold to the upper road, and in every way follow justice and wisdom."* [1]

St Paul firmly believed in that platonic idea. As we said, his interpretation of the message of Jesus and the Kingdom of God was actually based on the concept of an immortal soul.

Other theologians came up with all kinds of surreal theories about what happens to our souls when we die. Martin Luther espoused the idea that the soul went to sleep and remained asleep until doomsday. Locke thought that both body and soul die and then they are both resurrected (thnetopsychism). Many of them, including Priestley and Tyndale, believed in the resurrection of the dead.

The Pauline doctrine of the Catholic Church and other Christian Churches is of course that the individual soul is immortal. That is how humans can go to Heaven, or Hell, or Purgatory.

I would venture that St Paul did not misconstrue the original meaning of the Book of Genesis that Adam and Eve were animals who would die and that would be the end of it. I would say he understood 'you would surely die' to mean that human beings would die from then on, as Adam and Eve continued living and God could not have been wrong. Paul added that, if they were good, Jesus Christ would give their souls an immortal life in Heaven. But then, the other side of the coin —which I try to explain—was that prior to the expulsion they would have needed to be immortal (?).

In any case, had Paul given the Book of Genesis the interpretation intended by the scribes who wrote the allegory, he could have given Adam & Eve a soul afterwards. Perhaps... — as a way to find a solution to the difficult question. The problem with that interpretation is that St Paul probably wanted a clean break from the animal origin of the species to suit the semi-divine nature of human beings (as God had created man in His own image). They could have a messiah who was also the Son of God. It is difficult to tell if he wanted that and misconstrued the myth or if he really misinterpreted it. In any case, he came up with something more spiritual than what was in the Old Testament.

As we have said, some Greek philosophers (Plato), in a most civilised fashion, believed humans had an immortal soul. St Paul introduced an individual immortal soul based on Plato's but added details of his own to fit his Christian doctrine. Humans are better than and separate from all other animals. The Sadducees, who were the most important Jewish community, rejected the idea of the immortal soul then and Jews have rejected it ever since.

Aristotle thought we had souls, but mortal ones, like all other animals. Much later, St Thomas Aquinas went one step further and specified that only humans have immortal souls. He said that animals have souls that are mortal. These are the sort of decisions that plague Christian theology. However, we had become separated from our fellow creatures in the animal kingdom at a much earlier stage. St Thomas Aquinas, in that respect followed what had been said before him. And every time you make a decision like that you have to explain the whys and the wherefores, and that is not always an easy task. What follows never, never, makes a lot of sense.

Once St Paul had decided that humans don't die because, through Jesus, they are entitled to everlasting life in Heaven, the individual immortal soul became a very important part of Christian doctrine. Only humans have souls (actually at one point in time, after Columbus discovered America, there were debates as to whether Amerindians had souls).

Through St Paul's Christian idea though, even if you were a slave, or very poor, or sick, you still had a chance of eternal bliss. You only had to be an individual. Paul was a salesman, and he sold hope. Very successfully, I might add.

The notion of the immortal soul spread with Christianity. St Paul was indeed the one who sold the immortal dream to the masses.

If we depart from the fact that all animals are alive—i.e., that they have a *nephesh*, according to the Hebrews—, then what Adam and Eve acquired in the Garden of Eden was what the Greeks called *psyche*, what St Paul imagined as the individual immortal soul, and what we now call consciousness.

Unsurprisingly, St Paul's notion of soul was kind of Greek in that it was individual and immortal. He was a Hellenistic Jew. His images, adopted by the Fathers of the Church meant that Christianity was going on its own way, separate from Judaism. Christianity was going to be a religion of Gentiles.

CHRISTIANITY AND JUDAISM

Saul of Tarsus, who would later become St Paul was, above all, a Jew. His beginnings were the beginnings of a Jew. When he said that he wanted to separate his sect—that of Jesus—from Judaism (i.e., that he was going to accept Gentiles and reject the concept of circumcision), what he did resulted in an evolutionary process. That is, that Christianity was not created from zero. There are many common background points with Judaism. Christianity was created on the basis of the *Tanach*, the Bible of the ancient Hebrews.

In that sense, both religions base their faith on the *Tanach*, the book that has been the most influential book in the world. But differences of interpretation between Christianity and Judaism are huge. And all of them have to do with St Paul.

The interpretation the Jews gave to it relates to God, the land of Israel and the chosen people. It is a collection of stories of the Jewish nation. The Torah constitutes the absolute law for the Jews as ordered by God. That part (apart from the Talmud) is a guide on how to live as a Jew. The creation of humanity and the Myth of the Garden of Eden are not as important, for instance as the faith Abraham had and that he had to obey Yahweh and that he would become the forefather of a great nation. Jews do not believe in salvation simply because they do not believe in the individual soul or the afterlife.

Christians believe the Old Testament tells an unfinished story that can only be completed by reading the New Testament. Adam and Eve's loss of innocence, their disobedience, the sin and its punishment, have to end up in a story of forgiveness, redemption and salvation, that only arrives with the life, death and resurrection of Jesus of Nazareth. The explanation for everything resides in the individual soul.

ST JOHN THE BAPTIST

If there is an important person in Jesus's spiritual life, that person has to be the Baptist. Jesus' ministry commenced when he was thirty or thirty-one years old, after he heard about John a strange charismatic preacher who was baptising people on the other side of the River Jordan.

What the Gospels say is that John was the son of Zacharias, of Abia, and Elizabeth, descended from Aaron, who was also a relative of Mary, the mother of Jesus. Both of John's parents descended from priestly families and were a devout couple. They lived in the hills of Judah, near Hebron. Elizabeth had been barren for a long time. One day, an angel appeared to Zacharias and told him that Elizabeth would have a son, who would be called John (that is, his name was divinely given) and would be *"filled with the Holy Ghost"* (Luke 1:15). He would not drink alcohol. According to legend, Herod the Great ordered that Zacharias be killed. Her husband's death forced Elizabeth to flee into the desert with her baby. Again, Luke says: *"And the childe grew, and waxed strong in spirit, and was in the deserts, till the day of his shewing vnto Israel"* [1] The whole story of the killing of Zacharias and the flight to the desert is somewhat controversial. What appears to be certain is that John was descended from priestly families.

John continued living in the wilderness for the rest of his life. According to Luke, John heard the word of God: *"And he came into all the countrey about Iordane, preaching the baptisme of repentance for the remissio of sinnes;"* [2]

John normally dressed in wild-looking clothes, made of camel's hair, and a leather belt. He ate locusts and wild honey. His type of rough attire is reminiscent of Elijah, the prophet described in the *Torah* that foreshadowed John. Baptism was basically immersion, and he was known as The Baptist, or He who Administers the Ritualistic Immersion. By this cleansing with water, the sins of the people were forgiven and the people entered the life of the community. Were they also given a name? According to the Roman Catholic Church, the outpouring of water on all their flesh signified the outpouring of the Holy Ghost.

There are things that are interesting about John the Baptist: one is that, even in the times of Jesus, that is, two thousand one hundred years ago, he was brought up and lived in the desert and wore very primitive clothing. That appears to have been accepted in Israel as something maybe not totally normal but not totally unusual either. He was not a hermit. Arguably, his mother had taken him to live in the desert as a child, as we said, after his father's death. Another interesting thing is the concept of baptism. Both customs (living rough and daily immersing themselves in water) were apparently shared by the Essenes, a very well known sect nowadays as a result of the fairly recent discovery of the Dead Sea Scrolls. Some go as far as to say that John was an Essene. That, again, is unlikely.

There have been other religions or cults with initiation rites that involved immersing in water. Apuleius (a Roman author who lived in the second century AD) describes one such rite as the introduction to the cult of Isis. Again, interestingly, Lucius, the main character of his book *Metamorphoses* or *The golden ass* is transformed into an animal (an ass) and then brought back to his human shape by Isis. That is, he recovered his human form and re-entered the human community with the help of a deity. This is reminiscent of what happens through baptism.

What sins was John the Baptist washing away? Well, there is no description of the sins or an idea of sin before Christianity, I believe. Was the original sin among them? That is, was there a similar concept in those days? Could he forgive the sins of the people? Baptism is a Christian sacrament whose intention is to forgive the Original Sin and to welcome the individual as a member of the Christian community. Maybe that explains the fact that the person who is baptised is given a name. A name is necessary in a community. The Gospel according to Mark says that John's baptism was "for the forgiveness of sins". Aslan believes Mark has retrofitted that notion onto the Torah: *"The unmistakable Christian nature of this phrase casts serious doubt on its historicity. It sounds more like a Christian projection upon the Baptist's actions, not something the Baptist would have claimed for himself though if that is true, it would be an odd statement for the early church to make about John: that he had the power to forgive sins, even before he knew Jesus."* [3] I believe the washing away of the body could not have been to forgive sins. It was probably closer to ritual immersions in other religions:

to welcome the individual into a spiritual community, or the spiritual world in general.

The fact that we have consciousness, that we are self-aware, creates a duality in human beings: there are some tendencies in us that are more physical and some that are more spiritual. In ancient times, humans appear to have been very aware of that duality. Romans described the duality in terms of our Apollonian (more spiritual) and Dionysiac (sensual, emotional and irrational) natures.

And that brings us back to the Original Sin. Christian theological doctrine would have us believe that humans are sinful because of Adam's fall from grace at the Garden of Eden. Was that the meaning of the myth as it was in the *Torah*?

Whatever the meaning of the myth and of John's ritual, the most important thing about John is that he appears to have been instrumental in inspiring Jesus to take up his ministry.

JESUS

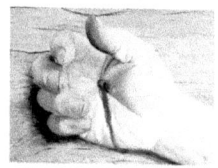

Throughout its history, Judaism had had holy men who were called 'prophets'. They would not necessarily predict future events, but their advice would be considered inspired by God and, as such, heeded, or at least respected. They were often outsiders, men with their own ethical and moral beliefs. Sometimes they would clash with the main religion, that of the Temple.

Jesus of Nazareth was a carpenter, or builder ('tekton' is the Greek term used in the New Testament), from the province of Galilee, in the North of Palestine. He lived in Nazareth but probably plied his trade in a big Graeco-Roman city: Sepphoris. After experiencing a revelation from God, like other mystics of the time, he began preaching and, according to his disciples, performing miracles. He gathered a band of followers who believed in him as a charismatic prophet. That little sect became the embryo of the Christian Church.

After Jesus' death, a Pharisee called Saul of Tarsus, later known as St Paul, joined the sect and became one of its main proselytisers. Paul, a very sophisticated man for the time, found himself among a group of illiterate leaders of a small sect. He was not interested in a small, peripheral Jewish sect. He wanted a universal religion. The best way to reach that goal, he decided, was to propose a Greek idea: eternal spiritual life. He eventually broke away from Judaism, but borrowed its God and the Jewish Bible, the *Tanakh*, and embellished the teachings of the *Torah* (the first five books, also called the *Pentateuch*) to suit the new doctrine. In doing all this Paul also gave humans the immortal soul they did not know they had.

There is no doubt about the power of Jesus, the man and his message. He has been the most influential figure in human history, whether some people like it or not. There is doubt, though, about the manner in which his message and his life were interpreted, misinterpreted, misrepresented, or generally embellished by the Evangelists, the Church, and Christianity in general.

Bhagwan Shree Rajneesh (aka Osho), an Indian "guru" of the second half of the twentieth century, believed that Jesus was an enlightened man and that he was totally misunderstood from the very beginning: *"Then what happens, how does this church come in? It happens because Jesus lives on a totally different plane of being, the plane of awareness – and those who listen to him, those who follow him, they live on the plane of sleep. Whatsoever they hear, interpret, it is interpreted through their own dreams – and whatsoever they create is going to be a sin".* [1] I would say he was not too far off the mark.

Unfortunately, Jesus left nothing in writing. Luke, in his Gospel, says that when he was twelve years old his parents found him in the Temple discussing religion with the doctors. No literacy is mentioned there; he was just a child asking questions and giving opinions. Later, Luke again says that when Jesus went back to Nazareth after being tempted by the Devil, he went to the synagogue and read a passage from the Scriptures. That is highly unlikely, as most of the population of Judea was illiterate at the time. He came from a very humble family and lived in a small town. Most probably Jesus, like his disciples, was illiterate. The fact that he left nothing in writing appears to confirm that hypothesis. That fact has to be placed in the context of the times and that he was in a primitive country that, itself, as we have said, was almost totally illiterate.

The only one of the group who left written documents was Paul. He was a total newcomer and did not even get to know Jesus. He joined the sect after Jesus died and wrote his Epistles decades later. The main documents we have about Jesus' life are the Gospels, written by the Evangelists, Matthew, Mark, Luke and John. Those are the four names, but we do not know much about their lives either. Again, the Gospels were written decades after the Epistles of Paul.

Aslan and many others doubt their historical accuracy. That is probably not the way to approach the Gospels. It is not quite reasonable to do that, as they are not meant to be biographical or historical records of the kind we know nowadays. Aslan says: *"These are not eyewitness accounts of Jesus's words and deeds recorded by people who knew him. They are testimonies of faith composed by communities of faith and written many years after the events they describe. Simply put, the gospels tell us about Jesus the Christ, not Jesus the man."* [2] We know that when stories are transmitted for many years, from one person to another and from one generation to another, there will be changes, heroes will become larger than life, anecdotes will be aggrandised, in summary, the stories will be naturally embellished. I must say,

I have to agree with Aslan to some extent, although the value of the Gospels is not exclusively historical.

Of course, the Evangelists give four different versions of the same official story. Their writings were chosen (canonised) among many to be part of the New Testament because they agreed with the main teachings of the Church. Mark's, Matthew's and Luke's (the *Synoptics*) were written more or less at the same time. The Gospel of John was written more than a century after Jesus' death. John is the one closest to Paul in terms of stressing the divinity of Jesus.

They all make an issue of proving that Jesus was at least the Messiah. John wants to prove that Jesus is not just the Christ, the Anointed One. Jesus is God.

One example that springs to mind: the prophecies stated that the Messiah had to come from the line of David and from the town of David, Bethlehem, so Matthew goes to great lengths to provide a genealogy of Jesus that begins in Abraham and goes, through David, to Joseph. *"Abraham begate Isaac, and Isaac begate Iacob... And Iacob begate Ioseph the husband of Mary, of whom was borne Iesus, who is called Christ."* [3]

There is one problem there already. Joseph may have descended from David, but Joseph was supposed to be only Jesus' putative father. Joseph was Jesus' father during Jesus' lifetime. We know that, according to the New Testament, the mother, Mary, was a virgin and the real father was the Holy Ghost. The Angel of God says that very clearly a few lines down: *"But while hee thought on these things, behold, the Angel of the Lord appeared vnto him in a dreame, saying, Ioseph thou sonne of Dauid, feare not to take vnto thee Mary thy wife; for that which is conceiued in her, is of the holy Ghost."* [4] In Luke I:28, the Angel tells Mary the same thing. She will conceive the son of the

Holy Ghost. And what happened to David's line? How was Jesus descended from David? Somehow, St Anna, Jesus' maternal grandmother, ended up being descended from David as well. Being a Jew, that would make sense, as Judaism is acquired through the maternal side. In any case, that is the sort of farfetchedness that plagues the New Testament. Then, you either believe or you don't.

Although he is called Jesus of Nazareth in various parts of the New Testament, and he lived in Nazareth most of his life, he was supposed to come from Bethlehem, because that would match what the prophets had said about the Messiah: that he was going to come from Bethlehem. Aslan points that out: *"Why, then, do Matthew and Luke and only Matthew (2:1-9) and Luke (2:1-21) claim that Jesus was born not in Nazareth but in Bethlehem, even though the name Bethlehem does not appear anywhere else in the entire New Testament (not even anywhere else in Matthew or Luke, both of which repeatedly refer to Jesus as "the Nazarean", save for a single verse in the gospel of John (7:42)?"* [5]

What is evident from the Gospels is that Jesus was a leader among men and a holy man. He was a man who had a message to convey. His message was religious, but not mainstream, or Temple-religious. The Temple had not served the Jews, and would not serve the Jews, against any of their oppressors, including the Romans. Jesus established himself as a charismatic, alternative figure. He promised he would liberate them from the yoke. But because he spoke in parables, as many wise men do and did in those days, he has been often misinterpreted. Aslan believes that he spoke of the liberation of Judea. That is probably true, but his message went obviously beyond that.

His message was indeed spiritual. In any case, Paul's reading of his message was spiritual... and then he added his own ideas to it, but always discussing the soul and the afterlife: *"For if ye liue after the flesh, ye shall die: but if ye through the spirit doe mortifie the deeds of the body, ye shall liue."* [6] At a time when pagan Romans were the overlords in Palestine, when there was little hope that things would change in anybody's lifetime, Paul's message was a message of eternal hope. The prospect of life in heaven was certainly a welcome ray of sunshine on the miserable lives of most peasants of the time, Jews and Gentiles alike.

When he was 32 years old, Jesus, apparently very impressed by John the Baptist, went to see him and he was indeed baptised by him in the river Jordan. The Gospels say that the Holy Ghost, in the shape of a dove, descended upon Jesus, and that the Baptist said *"This was he of whom I spake. He that commeth after me, is preferred before me, for he was before me."* [7] Later, Luke states *"And Iesus being full of the holy Ghost, returned from Iordane, and was led by the spirit into the wildernesse"*. There, he was tempted by the Devil and after returning, triumphant, he commenced his ministry.

Jesus had twelve disciples, who were probably meant to represent the twelve tribes of Israel. He chose the little coastal town of Capernaum as his base, and his preaching drew huge crowds of followers. According to the Gospels, he healed the sick, performed exorcisms and made miracles. The Evangelists give many examples of his miraculous deeds.

Jesus, in his speeches, made frequent references to the "Kingdom of God", and he promised his listeners that those among them who believed in him would get to see the kingdom. It was never clear if he meant the afterlife and heaven, or if he only meant a kingdom where poor peasants would not go hungry any more, where the sick would be healed, even where the dead would not necessarily be dead forever. Mark gives an example where he resuscitates the child of a woman who had faith that he could do it: *"And they laughed him to scorne but when he had put them all out, hee taketh the father and the mother of the damosell, and them that were with him, and entre in where the damosell was lying. And he took the damosell by the hand and said vnto her, Talitha cumi, which is, being interpreted, Damosell (I say vnto thee) Arise. And straightway the damosell arose, and walked, for shee was of the age of twelue yeeres : and they were astonished with a great astonishment."* [8] Jesus was promising that there would be changes coming soon and, according to the Gospels, he showed with his miracles how the changes would be.

There is no doubt that he was an exceptionally wise teacher. When you want to teach something, demonstration works wonders. And Jesus literally worked wonders. Parables, which he used very frequently, operated like shorthand. Instead of explaining, Jesus told stories (and performed miracles). The only problem with his method was that the interpretations of his stories and sayings differed quite markedly, as we know. His speeches and his actions combined provided a very powerful picture that people obviously believed. And they were keen to hear whatever Jesus had to say.

His Capernaum ministry was very successful, so he travelled to different areas, including outside of Judea. He went to Tyre and Sidon, in Phoenicia. Then he headed East of the Jordan, to a town called Caesarea Philippi. Jesus wanted to know what people thought of him. He sought reassurance from his disciples: *"... saying vnto them, Whom doe men say that I am?... And Peter answered and saith vnto him, 'Thou art the Christ'."* [9] Well, according to Mark, during his lifetime he was at least the anointed one, the chosen one. He was the "Christ".

For Passover, Jesus went to Jerusalem mounted on a donkey. The people of Jerusalem welcomed him with palms, which he enjoyed, but he did not like what he saw in the Temple. The money changers were doing their business, as people had to pay for their sacrifices and they had to pay not in Roman coins but in Temple shekels. Jesus confronted them; he yelled that they had made a den of thieves out of the Temple, and he overturned the tables of the dove sellers. That outburst was probably the one that would cost him his crucifixion. Caiaphas, the High Priest, was not going to tolerate that kind of behaviour in his Temple.

During the Passover dinner, Jesus announced that one of his disciples, who was present then, would betray him. He was referring to Judas Iscariot. After the meal they all went to Gethsemani where he asked the disciples to sit and wait for him while he prayed. When he was praying and the disciples had gone to sleep, lots of soldiers with swords turned up at Gethsemani, led by Judas. Judas had told them that they would recognise Jesus because he would give him a kiss. After Judas kissed him, the soldiers took him to Caiaphas, who was the one who had ordered his arrest. Caiaphas interrogated him.

But because Caiaphas did not have the authority to judge him as this was Roman-occupied Judea, Jesus had to be taken then to the Roman prefect, Pontius Pilate. Pontius, again, interrogated him. And then he offered the people the choice of sparing Jesus and crucifying another prisoner, Barabbas. Mark tells us that the people said that Jesus should be crucified. That version of the event has been used against the Jews for over two thousand years. It was a strange development, as crucifixion was a Roman punishment. Jesus was judged and found guilty by Roman authorities. And the crime he allegedly committed was that of rebellion. According to what was written on the cross, his crime was that he wanted to be King of the Jews (Iesus Nazarenvs Rex Iudaeorum/ INRI).

Aslam doubts the veracity of the episode and provides a plausible answer: *"Why would Mark have concocted such a patently fictitious scene, one that his Jewish audience would immediately have recognized as false? The answer is simple: Mark's audience was in Rome, where he himself resided. His account of the life and death of Jesus of Nazareth was written mere months after the Jewish Revolt had been crushed and Jerusalem destroyed".* [10]

Jesus was then scourged and crucified as he was a troublemaker and a rebel against the Temple and Rome. He was taken to a place called the Golgotha ("hill of skulls", in Aramaic) where other "bandits" would be crucified with him. The disciples had all left and were in hiding out of fear of being crucified themselves. Only two women, Mary Magdalene and Mary, his mother, were with him until the bitter end. All in all, his ministry had lasted one year. When he died he was only thirty-three years old.

The four Evangelists agree that Joseph of Arimathea, a member of the Sanhedrin and a follower of Jesus, was the person who took charge of Jesus' burial. Joseph bought a shroud to cover the body and lent his own family tomb, which was a cave-like sepulchre carved out of a rock, to bury him. What happened afterwards is one of the main tenets of the Catholic Church, and of Christianity in general. According to John, the Evangelist, Mary Magdalene went to visit the tomb and found it empty. She went to where the disciples were and asked them to come to the sepulchre with her. Peter and another disciple went and found the tomb empty. Mary Magdalene looked in and saw two angels sitting where Jesus' body had been lying. And then she saw him and Jesus talked to her and told her to tell the disciples what had happened. Jesus Christ had been resurrected, body and soul.

ST PAUL

*B*efore we attempt to explain the role of St Paul in the development or creation of Christianity, perhaps we should briefly analyse the state of Judaism during the life of Jesus.

It was a time of great change in Palestine, a time of fluidity and as it often happens different, opposing, factions coexisted during the period of crisis. In the case of Judaism, there were basically three layers that are vital to understanding how Christianity came about and who Paul was: 1) There was the Temple (the Sadducees and the Priestly class), who stuck to the original Judaism of animal sacrifices to Yahweh and the classic interpretation of Scriptures; 2) there were the Pharisees, who were a new sect (plus the Essenes to a lesser extent) that interpreted and analysed the Hebrew Bible in a much more rigorous manner. After the destruction of the second Temple by the Romans under Titus in AD70, they became the main exponent of Judaism – and the current Rabbis and their Talmud and Mishna are in a way, their descendants –; and 3) there were various exponents of what Geza Vermes calls "charismatic Judaism"; John the Baptist and Jesus of Nazareth were both exponents of that type of religious expression: holy men who healed the sick, performed miracles, prophesied and carried out exorcisms and resurrections (there were some among the Essenes as well); they had sometimes large numbers of followers and were traditionally considered new versions of prophets like Samuel, Elijah and Elisha, who had lived several centuries before. Aslan even says that *"John may have been an Essene"*.

What is quite clear is that Judaism was in a fluid state. The new currents of the religion rejected animal sacrifice as the main form of worship. The Sadducees and their Temple were on the wrong side of history. However, Paul, who had been a Pharisee, wanted to interpret that Jesus' sacrifice had occurred to make amends for the sins of humanity. Maybe that is what links the Temple with Christianity. That happens, as we said before, in a way in which Paul emphasises the cruelty of archaic religions and, at the same time, while killing God, speaks of the human being as an individual.

Both the Pharisees and the charismatic Jews were tolerated by the Sadducees, who vehemently opposed the notion of the immortal soul. All of them had access to the Temple. We know the rest: the Sadducees ceased to exist, the Pharisees metamorphosed into Rabbinic Judaism, and the charismatic Jews, or a branch of it, emerged as Christianity.

It is possible that Saul, or Paul, who was a Jew of the diaspora and a survivor of crises, belonged to all three streams of Judaism at one time or another. And the sequence would have been the logical one: Sadducee > Pharisee > Christian. By 33AD, before Christ's death he was a Pharisee.

Paul was much more sophisticated than any of the apostles (he was not one of them, even though he later aspired to be recognised as one). He was also more educated than Jesus, whom he had not met and who, as we have said, was most probably illiterate. Paul could read and write, and spoke three languages and, in terms of doctrine, his Epistles, or letters, are among the most influential chapters of the New Testament.

Let us go back to the historical facts. After Jesus died, many of the apostles left Jerusalem and spread in all directions. Only a few remained in Jerusalem and those who stayed later became the main Christian Council.

Paul was a native of Tarsus, the capital of Cilicia, which in those days was part of Hellenistic Rome. The Empire had granted citizenship rights to the citizens of Tarsus. Paul was a Jew, and a Pharisee, and he was also a Roman citizen. He could speak Greek (Demotiki), Latin and Aramaic. At the time of Jesus's death he was in Jerusalem, where he had lived for some time and, according to his own account, he was among the most fanatical Pharisees who persecuted the disciples of Jesus. Apparently, he participated in St Stephen's martyrdom. Later on, when he converted, he became as fanatical a Christian as he had been a Pharisee.

Whether the notion of the individual immortal soul preceded Saul/St Paul among the Pharisees or it was the other way around is really immaterial. Perhaps the Pharisees had already accepted the idea. It so happens that when he became a Christian (when he "created" Christianity), the immortal soul turned up as part of the new religion. It followed him like his shadow. Paul's Hellenistic background, I believe, was an indication that he had come into contact with Plato's ideas about the immortal soul. Was that a coincidence? I don't think so.

As an educated person and one who had lived in cities all his life, it was very easy for somebody like Paul to idealise human virtues. From predicating that humans had an immortal soul to predicating that a human being was divine there was just one step. Paul was not one for half measures. He went the whole hog. Of course, it took another two hundred odd years before it became an official part of Christian dogma.

There would have been three logical steps in this stream of thought, although this is just a hypothesis: 1) Humans are not animals. > 2) Humans, as opposed to animals, have an individual immortal soul. > 3) A human can be a god. Well, maybe here we can see a logical progression.

This last point was not altogether original, as Roman emperors had already been totally deified. The difference is that Rome's religion was a polytheistic one, with several gods in their Pantheon, whereas Paul proposed a progression: a human could be divine in a monotheistic religion derived from Judaism.

The story goes that Paul's conversion happened when he was on the road to Damascus to destroy the Christian community there. He saw a very bright light and heard a voice that asked him:

"Saul, Saul, why persecutest thou me?

And he said, Who art thou Lord?

And the Lord said, I am Iesus whom thou persecutest..." [1]

The way St Paul operated after that is in line with a definite shift towards charismatic Judaism, (which would eventually lead him away from Judaism and into the creation of Christianity). According to Geza Vermes: *"The personal impact of the envoy of God plays a paramount role in charismatic Judaism. Contact with him is an essential stepping-stone in the march towards the Deity... and the entire Pauline and Johannine literature, not to mention centuries of theological effort deployed by the Christian church, sought to expound Jesus' relation to God and the redeeming character of his life and death.*

In short, without a proper grasp of charismatic Judaism it is impossible to understand the rise of Christianity." [2] As we can see, the idea of the Anointed One, the Chosen One, the Christos, was pivotal in Charismatic Judaism. Although Jesus retained the name Christ by becoming not just Jesus the Christ, but Jesus Christ, the whole idea of envoy disappeared and he actually became the Son of God. He became an integral part of the Trinity or the Godhead.

Redemption, the payment of a ransom to liberate oneself of a debt, a concept closely related to the sacrifices of the Sadducees, the scapegoat, the sacrificial lamb; related even to Isaac's sacrifice, that his father, Abraham, was prepared to carry out to appease God, to show his love for God, became a central concept of Pauline Christianity, albeit in a more sophisticated form. The Son of God sacrificed himself to deliver humanity from sin. All humans, fallen after Adam and Eve's disobedience were redeemed by Jesus' goodness.

Saul went on to Damascus but he had already converted. No Christians were killed there.

One could be very cynical about this whole episode. St Paul was a leader of men. He was ambitious. He had new ideas and saw that there was this opening in what originally was just a new form of charismatic Judaism. The Christian community in Jerusalem, headed by James, Jesus' brother, appeared to have no big plans. The Council of Jerusalem was going nowhere. They were all simple villagers.

St Paul travelled extensively after his conversion, first from Antioch to Cyprus, then to Anatolia and then to many other cities during the period of his missionary endeavours. His message changed as he proselytised among Jews first and, later, increasingly among Gentiles. One of the major centres of his work was Antioch. On his second missionary journey, it was obvious that St Paul's message was deviating more and more away from Judaism. On his return to Palestine he discussed circumcision at a meeting of the Apostolic Council. He had at least two major arguments with the leaders of the movement, James and Peter.

There were all kinds of political differences between St Paul and the Council. Paul saw the future as a break away from Judaism. James, Peter and the rest of the Council wanted to remain within the Jewish fold, at most become a Jewish sect. Nothing was certain. The situation appeared to be fairly unstable for the new movement. Jesus had not quite respected the food prohibitions of the Jews, but under St Paul, the issue of circumcision was the one that would become pivotal in terms of staying Jewish or not. The conversion of Gentiles was at stake.

The Council of Jerusalem sent delegations to St Paul's congregation in Galatia and to other places where he had been preaching. They were supposed to correct St Paul's views on the doctrine, especially about the Messiah and the Laws of Moses (the *Torah*).

Aslan describes how St Paul reacted to these intrusions: *"Paul was incensed by these delegations, which he viewed, correctly, as a threat to his authority. Almost all of Paul's epistles in the New Testa-*

ment were written after the Apostolic Council and are addressed to congregations that had been visited by these representatives from Jerusalem... That is why these letters devote so much space to defending Paul's status as an apostle, touting his direct connection to Jesus, and railing against the leaders in Jerusalem..." [3]

Paul defended his teachings with vitriolic attacks against the Jerusalem Council and their representatives:

"10. As the trueth of Christ is in mee, no man shall † stop mee of this boasting in the regions of Achaia.

11. Wherefore? Because I loue you not? God knoweth.

12. But what I doe, that I wil doe, that I may cut off occasion from them which desire occasion, that wherein they glory, that they may bee found euen as we.

13. For such are false Apostles, deceitfull workers, transforming themselues into the Apostles of Christ.

14. And no marueile, for Sathan himselfe is transformed into an Angel of light." [4]

Christianity grew rapidly. St Paul saw very clearly that the future was indeed promising if he presented a more open, more inclusive message among the Gentiles, hence the discussion on circumcision. On his third missionary journey, Paul travelled around Galatia and Phrygia, and then to Ephesus, Macedonia and Achaea. After a conflict with a group of Asian Jews in Cesarea, Paul was jailed for two years. As a Roman citizen, he requested being sent to Rome to present his appeal to the Emperor. In Rome he preached for another two years. After that he went to Hispania, where he continued with his work. Eventually, during Nero's reign, he was decapitated for his evangelic activities.

Aslan examines how St Paul reacted to St Peter's teachings in Rome:

"It is difficult to know just how successful Peter had become in his task before Paul arrived. But according to 'Acts', the Hellenists in Rome reacted so negatively to Paul's preaching that he decided to cut himself off once and for all from his fellow Jews." [5]

The die had been cast. That was the end of the Jewish journey for St Paul and for Christianity. St Paul focused his preaching on the Gentile community. He was, and remains, the most influential Christian theologian. There is no doubt that his activities and ideas changed the direction of Christianity, mostly away from Judaism, of which he reneged with a passion, especially concerning circumcision: *"Beware of dogs, beware of euill workers: beware of the concision."* [6]

Christianity would continue to grow. St Paul had done something much more transcendental than breaking away from Judaism and creating a new religion. He had added a new spirituality to the only primitive monotheistic religion in the world and had come up with a very powerful formula: a more spiritual monotheism.

Rubenstein has similar views: *"What most pagan leaders – even those as far-seeing as Diocletian – could not comprehend was the fact that the Christians had not merely added another god to the pantheon. They had redefined religion itself."* [7]

Paul cannot be any clearer than in Corinthians: *"Who also hath made vs able ministers of the New Testament, not of the letter, but of the spirit: for the letter killeth, but the spirit giueth life"… How shall not the ministration of the spirit be rather glorious?"* [8] When he talks about the letter, he is referring to the *Torah* as interpreted by the Sadducees. The difference between the Temple and Christianity.

With the benefit of hindsight it is possible to say now that Christianity was the obvious religious match for the Roman Empire, which covered basically most of the known world. Centuries later it would help Constantine unite the Empire politically and religiously for a long time to come. Later still, Theodosius would declare it the official religion of the Roman Empire. Christianity had come of age.

At the risk of oversimplifying the issue, let us try to summarise what happened: St Paul, a Jew and a Pharisee, converted to a charismatic sect of Judaism that was more spiritual than the Temple or any other sect as far as we know. Paul made Christianity even more spiritual. That should come as no surprise. He was a Hellenist, a Jew of the diaspora. Greek philosophers had been playing with the idea of the soul for some time and he had probably come into contact with the concept. He went for an individual immortal soul and adapted it to the doctrine of the new religion.

From a cynical point of view, it is quite possible that St Paul used the life of Jesus opportunistically in order to implement his own ideas about a less pragmatic, more spiritual religion. Osho believes that he was not altogether sincere about Jesus: *"In his epistles St. Paul uses 'in Christ' one hundred and sixty-four times. He must have been a little doubtful about it. 'In Christ... in Christ... in Christ...' one hundred and sixty-four times! It is too much. Once would have been enough. Even once is more than enough. It should be your being that shows you live in Christ – and then there is no need to say it".*[9]

A well-travelled, educated man, he soon realised that the ethnic restrictions and prohibitions of Judaism would be a liability to his sect. That was in stark opposition to the members of the Council of Jerusalem, who, I repeat, were illiterate Galileans. Their views were parochial to say the least. Paul did away with circumcision and other impediments and accepted Gentiles with open arms. *"There is neither Iewe, nor Greeke, there is neither bond nor free, there is neither male nor female: for ye are all one in Christ Jesus."* [10] It is obvious that he was very convincing and very successful at proselytising. After some negative reactions that he had at the beginning, and seeing that he was gaining new adepts wherever he went, the Christian Council of Jerusalem had to accept his ideas. The new sect retained the God of the Jews and the Jewish Bible. The *Tanakh* carried the authority of centuries of existence. They believed in Yahweh. Those were the religious elements Paul had. Only for them to become more Christian he needed to make them more universal. *"For there is no difference betweene the Iew and the Greeke : for the same Lord ouer all, is rich vnto all, that call vpon him"* [11]. Rather than creating everything from scratch, he reinterpreted the *Tanakh*, especially the Book of Genesis, in such a fashion that it would match his new emphasis on spirituality. That new spirituality, somehow, needed a clean break from the animal origins that were described in the *Torah*. Adam and Eve became human beings without any ancestors. Paul denied them a navel.

DID WE NEED A HUMAN GOD?

"The greatest mystery is not that we have been flung at random between the profusion of matter and of the stars, but that within this prison we can draw from ourselves images powerful enough to deny our nothingness."

- **Andre Malraux**

*A*mong the many ways Christianity had to 'deny our nothingness', to make humans important and provide hope of immortality, it appears to have chosen the least logical one, the one that was the most difficult to explain, hence all the "mysteries", all the unanswered questions. We could have been *"primus inter pares"*, first among equals. Maybe we did not need a human deity. Arius had a more rational answer. Nevertheless, that is the way things went.

Centuries passed between the Old and the New Testament. As we shall see, the Hebrew Bible, (or *Tanakh*, or *Mikra*) is an anthology of oral traditions conceived during prehistoric times and later written down. It thus became a quasi-historical document. The scribes of King Hezekiah apparently began compiling it for the first time in the 8th century BC (although there are various theories as to the date). The New Testament was written in the 1st and 2nd centuries AD and finally compiled in the 4th century AD, that is, quite a few centuries later. In the intervening centuries, humanity had advanced a great deal. Humans had built great cities, like Rome, Athens and Alexandria, had designed and constructed grand buildings and monuments, and amazing feats of engineering like aqueducts, bridges and roads. Enormous ships criss-crossed the Mediterranean, the *Mare Nostrum* of the Romans. Rome had a living god, the emperor.

Humans were magnificent creatures. Divinity among humans was indeed possible. At that point the position of Christianity must have turned one hundred and eighty degrees away from the position of the *Torah*. The blurry idea of a remote human/animal ancestor gave way to the certainty of a human/god.

God could live among us. Ours was a very large and unknown universe. The stars shone tiny in the night sky. Our planet was the centre of the cosmos. That was very clear for everyone to see. As we have said, geo-centricity would not be questioned until fourteen centuries later, when Copernicus posited the concept of heliocentrism. The Earth was only a minor planet orbiting the sun. Galileo Galilei proved it some years later. But until then humans, in their minds, were indeed at the centre of Creation.

I believe that the total separation of humans from animals was a step necessary towards the deification of Jesus. Had humans been mere animals, it would have been very difficult to justify the existence of a god among us. No doubt, all the measures taken by St Paul and the Church in order to distance Jesus from a normal human conception were based on that notion. He was meant to be above the rest of humanity while still being human.

Early Christianity was moving towards deification but had not quite reached that stage before the Council of Nicaea. Geza Vermes gives an account of the distinctive beliefs of early Christians:

"Set against mainstream Judaism, three distinctive teachings secured recognizable identity for the Christian movement: the Kingdom of God; the crucified, risen and exalted Messiah; and the Parousia or second coming of Christ." [1]

It is not one hundred percent sure that St Paul was the one who introduced the concept of Jesus as a supernatural, divine being. Maybe he said that Jesus acquired the status of 'Son of God' after his resurrection. But Paul was definitely pointing towards deification. However, during the first century AD, the notion of Jesus as God appears not to have been totally secure. That would be fixed in Nicaea, centuries later. Vermes believes that Paul did not mean for Jesus to be deified: *"In fact, Paul never envisaged Jesus as fully sharing the nature of the Deity. When compared to God the Father, 'the Son' always occupies an inferior position in Pauline thought, although he stands far above ordinary humans. The co-equality of the divine persons is a concept that is still centuries away."* [2]

Many biblical experts nowadays appear to believe that there is a definite correlation between the Johannine and the Pauline positions. Maybe John went one tiny step further in the direction of the deification. His Gospel is clearly different from those of Matthew, Mark and Luke. John believed that Jesus was actually God. At the time, while the other, synoptic*, gospels called Jesus the "son of God", John called him simply God. The difference was barely noticeable then.

Elaine Pagels proposes that John actually followed in Paul's steps: *"Yet John, who wrote about a decade after Luke, opens his gospel with a poem which suggests that Jesus is not human at all but the divine, eternal Word of God in human form... The author whom we call John probably knew that he was not the first —and certainly not the only— Christian to believe that Jesus was somehow divine... Unlike Luke, who depicts Jesus as a man raised to divine status, John, as does the hymn Paul quotes, pictures him instead as a divine being who descended to earth —temporarily— to take on human form"* [3]

Cynically, I tend to see Paul as the first "believer" in Jesus's divinity.

But what is clear in my mind is that Bishop Irenaeus of Lyons was as instrumental as Paul and John in deciding about the deification of Jesus. He agreed with John that Jesus was indeed God. And he was the one who decided that John's gospel had to be included among the four that would become the basis of the Church's dogma. Origen Adamantios, and bishops Alexander, and Athanasius, all of them of Alexandria, would pick up the divinity banner later. The force of their commitment to the idea gave shape to what we now know as Christianity.

And Christianity followed Paul's idea of Genesis and adopted the view that human beings had always been separate from the rest of nature. Human beings were creators, very close to gods. Animal species were immutable. Human beings were separate and also immutable. Not only that: God was among us.

Was it an error? If it was, what is amazing is that an error of that magnitude could have prevailed for so long. What is also amazing is that after Darwin demonstrated evolution, and after irrefutable evidence, like fossils, and the amount of DNA we share with animals, there are still people in the twenty-first century who cling to the idea of Creation the way Paul saw it.

The understanding from then on was that humans were never animals. So much so that Christians came up with an interesting notion: all humans share the Original Sin. But that sin had nothing to do with our animal origins. According to the Church, it has to do with the sin committed by Adam and Eve (which sin was that? It appeared to them that it was pride/disobedience/ concupiscence (!)*). This is what they read from the Bible. However, that sin would be forgiven with baptism, that is the moment we are born into our spiritual society. The punishment for the original sin is that we die, but we are saved through the intervention of Jesus Christ and the Holy Spirit. The logical consequences of that dictum that we die but our soul may be saved (or damned) for all eternity are the concepts of the immortal soul and eternal life in heaven. It also means that hell had to be created as well for those who did not qualify for heaven. And, for some, the fate was purgatory. At that point, things became really complicated and they didn't make a lot of sense any more. In any case, the individuality of the soul, the consequences of which were barely noticeable then, made our individual actions incredibly important. Unlike the [rest of the] animals, we could make good and bad decisions and were accountable to God. We had free will. We could act in a good or a bad way and we had to face the consequences.

Elaine Pagels questions the validity of the Pauline interpretation of the Book of Genesis:

"For millennia, Jews and Christians have attempted to explain the mystery of human suffering as moral judgment– the price of Adam and Eve's sin. The creation story of Genesis, addressing the question Why do we suffer and why do we die?, makes the empirically absurd claim that death does not constitute the natural end of all lives but intruded upon our species solely because Adam and Eve made the wrong choice." [4]

In my view she errs when she adds "Jews and...". I do believe the authors of the *Torah* wrote something totally different from what Christians believe nowadays. The concepts of earthly death and sin and eternal life were definitely introduced by Christianity. If any of those concepts have passed on to some sects of Rabbinical Judaism it is by Christian influence, no doubt.

A bit like Goebbels used to say, the wrong interpretation had been repeated so many times that, even if absurd, it sounded true. It is, however, a New Testament interpretation.

As we said, St Augustine of Hippo equated the notion of Original Sin with concupiscence. Some Jewish theologians appear to have agreed with this, as did Martin Luther and John Calvin. Yes, sexual urges are part of our animal nature, but where does the *Torah's* version of the Garden of Eden, mention sex or concupiscence?

Human beings had discovered the concept of "spirit" or "soul". Whenever the word "spirit" appears in the Hebrew Bible, it refers to the breath of life, the spirit of Yahweh. In Christian texts it normally means the individual immortal soul.

However, the concept of an immortal soul also became present in latter Judaism (the Pharisees/ Rabbis again?).

Some critics of the Bible find the New Testament logically more acceptable than the Old Testament. I find that hard to believe. Professor Dawkins is one of them: *"Well, there's no denying that, from a moral point of view, Jesus is a huge improvement over the cruel ogre of the Old Testament. Indeed Jesus, if he existed (or whoever wrote his script if he didn't) was surely one of the great ethical innovators of history."* [5]

Even from a cynical perspective, Dawkins keeps on taking Yahweh out of context. He is not sure about the existence of Jesus either. The way I see it, a God that created the Universe even if he began as the ineffable, albeit exclusive, El, later Yahweh, of the Hebrews is much more credible as a god than a 'divine' man, regardless of how extraordinary that man was.

Also, without going into Jesus's divinity, how did Christianity become a new religion, separate from Judaism? Could Jesus have foreseen anything like the New Testament? Was he trying to establish a new religion? We know it wasn't quite like that. Vermes has a very clear answer based on the many eschatological references of the apostles: *"In short, the religion of Jesus was the religion of Moses and the biblical prophets, but a religion adapted for the requirements of the final age in which he and his generation believed they found themselves."* [6]

Jesus appears to have added a spirituality that nobody had quite advocated until then, perhaps with the exception of John the Baptist. We have to remember that Jesus went to Judea, to the shores of the Jordan River to be baptised by him. But Vermes is even more specific when he states: *"The religion proclaimed by Jesus was a wholly theocentric one in which he played the role of the man of God par excellence, the prophet of prophets, the shepherd of the flock, the leader, revealer and teacher without being himself in any sense the object of worship as he later became in the fully fledged Christianity created by Paul and John, and especially from the second century onwards."* [7]

ARIANISM, THE COUNCIL OF NICAEA AND THE DEIFICATION OF JESUS

*J*n the fourth century AD the main problem facing the Fathers of the Church was deciding whether Jesus was really God or not. And whether, as God, he was equal to the Father. That was a decision that had to be made. It had not been revealed. They had to interpret the New Testament and decide. Richard Rubenstein summarises the conundrum:

"How could one be a Christian and not believe that Christ was God incarnate? The Arians had an answer. To them, Jesus was a person of such sublime moral accomplishments that God adopted him as His Son, sacrificed him to redeem humanity from sin, raised him from the dead and granted him divine status. Because of his excellence, he became a model of righteous behavior for us. And because his merit earned the prize of immortality, the same reward was made available to other human beings, provided they model themselves after him." [1]

According to Arius, even though Jesus was not totally divine, he provided hope for everyone. A subordinate Jesus was a logical way of keeping real monotheism and maintaining God as the invisible being that had spoken to Moses. Jesus Christ, on the other hand, the anointed one was a lesser deity but still a model for all humans. We could all aspire to perfection by emulation.

Arius was a presbyter who lived in Alexandria during the 3rd and 4th centuries AD. Not much is known about him personally, except that he was tall and thin, with a long grey beard, and that he was the typical holy man of the time. Three centuries earlier, Paul had decided on a clean break from Judaism. Arius advocated a smoother transition.

Arius believed there was a time when only the Father existed, a time before Jesus was created from nothing, *ex nihilo*. Compared to the Christian God, for instance, the gods of the Roman and Greek pantheons were not eternal, they were just immortal, therefore not true gods. The God of Jews and Christians, Yahweh, was eternal. He was the one who had created the universe from nothing.

According to Arius, the fact that Jesus had been created from nothing was a major obstacle in terms of his divinity. Jesus was part of creation. Not being eternal, Jesus could not be fully divine. Arius saw the Trinity as a misrepresentation of monotheism. What he believed was that God the Father was the main divine being and that Jesus was something akin to a demigod, a lesser god. Arius accepted that both Father and Son were divine, but each in a different way. Unfortunately, most of his teachings were destroyed, so we do not have many details except some accounts of the debates at the Council of Nicaea.

By the time Arius commenced preaching his ideas, which would later become the Arian heresy, the nature of the essence of the Son had been seriously debated for many decades. Obviously, Jesus' divinity —of which Paul gave us the first glimpse and which John adopted wholeheartedly in its fully-fledged version— presented serious problems that had to be resolved before a decision on the theology of the new Church could be reached.

Nowadays when we make reference to an argument concerning topics that are involved, intricate, complicated, we say that the argument is 'Byzantine'. The Church councils went to amazing lengths to explain the relationship between the members of the godhead. Eventually, centuries later, the Eastern Orthodox Church separated from the Roman Catholic Church over the word *"filioque"* (through the son). The question at that point was whether the Holy Spirit was divine through the Son or on its own merit.

There was no way to explain how Jesus could be God the Creator if he was not eternal. We know that he died. His body died like that of any other human being. But then, according to the Church, he resurrected (because, as God, he could not die altogether).

CONSTANTINE AND THE COUNCIL OF NICEA

In one of the corners of St Mark's Basilica, in Venice, there is a beautiful monument in the Byzantine style. Four men wearing crowns embrace. They are the Tetrarchs, and the monument symbolises their unity. For a brief period in the history of the Roman Empire, there were four monarchs (two Augusti and two Caesars).

Instituted by Diocletian in 297AD, the Tetrarchy lasted until 313AD, when only Constantine and Licinius remained as co-emperors of the West and East respectively. That situation would not last very long either. Inevitably one of them would claim the other side and would unite East and West into the all-powerful Roman Empire. That emperor was Constantine the Great, and the unification took place in 324AD.

The empire had been disintegrating for some time. Constantine took two important measures to arrest that disintegration. The first one was to convert to Christianity, as the number of the faithful had grown exponentially on both sides of the empire. At the Battle of Ponte Milvio, and following the advice of his old mentor, Bishop Hosius of Cordova, Constantine became a Christian. Having won the battle, he claimed that he had seen a cross in the sky and had heard the words *"Toutoi nika/ In hoc signo vincis"* (*"With this symbol you will win"*), but there are other versions, including that he had the initials of the word *Christos* emblazoned on the shields of his soldiers. The second measure was to move the imperial capital from Rome to his newly created city, Constantinople: the Empire needed a new lease on life.

Even before becoming sole Emperor, Constantine had managed to negotiate an end to the persecution of Christians. Later, Theodosius would declare that Christianity had become the official religion of the Roman Empire.

As we said, the growth of the Church had been amazing, and the bishops of the East wanted to meet in order to discuss several issues that were becoming problematic. One of them, of course, was Arianism. Bishop Alexander of Alexandria and other Nicene bishops asked Constantine to convene a Council.

Constantine sent his religious mentor, Hosius, to Alexandria. There, Hosius convinced the Eastern bishops to sign an anti-Arian pronouncement. He also excommunicated three Arian bishops, including Eusebius of Nicomedia, who was the most important leader among the Arian churchmen. The see of Eusebius's bishopric was Constantine's capital, and Eusebius was in very good terms with Constantine himself, so his excommunication was a bit of a bold move on the part of Hosius.

In any case, Constantine asked Hosius to preside over the Great Council of Bishops, which was to be held at Nicaea. Constantine decided on Nicaea after careful consideration of several other places. Nicaea was advantageous to the anti-Arian bishops. The Emperor had a palace there and he would be the main host of the meeting.

Constantine had been a tireless defender of Christianity, especially during the cruel persecutions Christians had suffered, so the bishops must have felt welcome at Nicaea. But because of that he was also in a position where he could influence the result of the meeting. According to Rubenstein:

"He agreed with Hosius that the dispute should be ended on terms favorable to Alexander and the anti-Arians" [1]

The bishops met for several weeks and debated, among other things the word *homoousios*, which roughly means "of the same substance". The idea was to decide whether Jesus was of the same substance as God the Father (or not).

The main opponent of Arianism, Athanasius of Alexandria, a disciple of Bishop Alexander of Alexandria, could not accept a watered-down version of the divinity of Christ. Jesus Christ was God. Anything less was a heresy. Jewish theology was totally unimportant, Judaism was offensive and anti-Christian.

The version of the Nicene bishops was that St Paul had pronounced himself in favour of Jesus' divinity and had opposed strictly following the principles of the *Torah*, as Jesus had not done himself: *"For Christ is the end of the Law for righteuousnes to euery one that beleeueth"* [2] 'The Law' here means the Torah. A strong God would mean a strong Church and a strong Empire. Constantine, of course, found the concept very attractive. He was mainly interested in a united and powerful Roman Empire.

At the Council, the Trinitarian bishops attacked Arius's ideas with incredible passion.

Rubenstein summarises the questions that arose from Arius' teachings:

"All Christians believed that Jesus's sacrifice redeemed humanity. What God did for the Son by resurrecting him and granting him immortality He could do for us as well, provided that we became new people in Christ. But if Jesus was not God by nature – if he earned his deification by growing in wisdom and virtue – why, so can we all. The Good News of the Gospels is that we also are God's potential Sons and Daughters. How then, is Christ essentially different or superior to us? And if he is not, what does it mean to call ourselves Christians?" [3]

That was the position of the anti-Arian bishops.

Emperor Constantine had ordered the Council to decide on the creed of the Church. Even though the bishops were supposed to be reasonable and show consideration to each other, the Council was not an example of civility or rational debate by any means.

Aslan describes the main deliberations of the Council:

"The bishops were not to disband until they had resolved the theological differences among them, particularly when it came to the nature of Jesus and his relationship to God. Over the centuries since Jesus's crucifixion, there had been a great deal of discord and debate among the leaders of the church over whether Jesus was human or divine. Was he, as those like Athanasius of Alexandria claimed, God incarnate, or was he, as the followers of Arius seemed to suggest, just a man – a perfect man, perhaps, but a man nonetheless?" [4]

Arius of Alexandria, as we have seen, believed that Christ was not of the same essence as God the Father and that he had not been eternal. Most bishops supported this. Rubenstein says that the Council was *"... the last point where Christians with strongly opposed views acted civilly towards each other"*. Many others disagree. There is a version of events, probably apocryphal, that has Bishop Nicholas of Myra (yes, St Nicholas, aka Santa Claus) punch or slap Arius and kick him out of the Council. Arius did not even take part in the deliberations, as he was not a bishop. Eventually, he was excommunicated. Some years later, at a Council held in Constantinople in 336, he died in rather strange circumstances, probably poisoned.

After several amendments, the document reflected the Emperor's and Hosius' anti-Arian views. Consequently, the Council of Nicaea made some primary choices in 325 AD that would prove very difficult in terms of explaining other elements of the Christian doctrine. Goodbye monotheism? The result is the Holy Trinity as we know it. A mystery, but a very interesting one at that.

Jesus could have been just another prophet. However, it was decided that Jesus was the Son of God. He could be. Human beings were so close to being gods. Human beings were above the rest of creation. With Paul, Christianity was in the process of becoming anthropocentric. After the Council of Nicaea, Christianity would become totally so. Did the idea result from a misinterpretation? Was the *Torah* misconstrued? Maybe. Jesus was not the only one who called God his Father. Geza Vermes explains clearly:

"In brief, it can be safely concluded that calling on God as Father was traditional in Jewish circles; it was not, as has been repeatedly claimed by ill-informed or biased New Testament interpreters, an

innovation introduced and practised by Jesus, and handed down only in the circle of his followers." [5]

There were many different and contrasting accounts of what Jesus had said and done and what had happened during his lifetime. The Church began culling, almost straight away, what was not acceptable as dogma, what were described as "heresies". Once you make a choice, the process, of course, limits your account of the events that follow. As we have discussed, Paul gave his version.

If you cannot beat them, join them. Constantine became a Christian and, in doing so, he bought extra time for the Roman Empire. In fact he bought an extra thousand years of Roman domination of the world. Christendom ceased to be a concept and became the known world.

INDIVIDUALITY & THE CHURCH

THE SEED OF CHANGE FROM WITHIN

*A*s we have said, the individual was important to Christians from the very beginning, when they were told their individual souls would go to heaven, with God. And the concept of the individual's direct contact with the Divinity crops up countless times after that, and not necessarily from rebel priests, as some Protestants want to believe.

Joachim da Fiore predicted that direct kind of contact centuries before Luther. Joachim was a 12th century Calabrian preacher and theologian who travelled to the Holy Land, eventually deciding to become a monk.

Extremely popular and well-connected, he was counsellor of Margaret of Navarre, founded an abbey, and was in very good terms with the Pope and with several kings and queens. He had a theory, of the Three Ages, the last of which would be the Age of the Holy Spirit. During that age, individuals would be able to directly contact the Holy Spirit. He prophesied that the Kingdom of the Holy Spirit would mean the end of organised religion. At that stage, he said that anyone who would bring the Christian message would be the equivalent to Jesus. The Church would then disappear.

The Catholic Church had several crises before the Reformation, and there were rebellious priests and monks before Martin Luther. From the second half of the fourteenth century to the first half of the fifteenth century, the papacy had to deal with the Western Schism, among other setbacks. During the years of the Schism the Church had three popes. The difference with other crises was that the Schism was mainly political and to do with personal ambitions. Corruption and immorality were endemic in the Church during those years. There were signs of discontent before Luther, but the Church suppressed them with an iron fist. The appearance of the Reformation was inevitable.

Girolamo Savonarola had entered the order of the Dominican friars in his native town of Ferrara, Northern Italy, in 1475. A smart friar, he was promoted very rapidly to important positions within the order until, in 1489, Lorenzo de Medici, on advice of his friend Pico della Mirandola author of the *Oration on the dignity of Man*, the Manifesto of the Renaissance, asked him to go to Florence.

Savonarola, a fiery eschatological preacher, commenced his sermons in 1490 and concentrated them on three prophesies: that the Church would undergo a major renovation, a denunciation of the clergy because they had strayed from the true worship; that Italy would suffer a terrible evil; and that those events would happen very soon.

The idea behind Savonarola's sermons was to establish a new 'theocratic' republic in Florence and to challenge the government of the Medici family and the papacy of Alexander VI.

After the death of Lorenzo the Magnificent, Piero de Medici accepted a humiliating treaty with Charles VIII of France, which resulted in the expulsion of the Medici family from the city at the end of 1494. While Florence was under French occupation, Savonarola took the opportunity to grab power and later negotiated a treaty with France. What followed was a strictly puritanical and moralistic regime that condemned self-indulgence and sex, and took a strict stance against immorality of any sort. In 1497 the citizens of Florence burnt anything that could induce to temptation and sin by means of huge 'bonfires of the vanities'. In the meantime, Savonarola kept on calling for changes in the Church. Pope Alexander VI made several unsuccessful attempts to reign him in, including consecrating him as a cardinal. The rebellious monk rejected all the advances of the Church and continued defiantly preaching against it very much like Luther some decades later. In the meantime, Charles VIII of France had signed a treaty with the Spanish monarch that left Florence without any international protection.

In 1497 Pope Alexander excommunicated the preacher. He accused him of heresy and of trying to introduce new doctrine, and labelled him a false prophet. The result was that on 23 May 1498 Girolamo Savonarola and two of his closest followers were hanged and burned at the stake. Their ashes were thrown in the Arno.

Savonarola's biggest mistake was not a theological one. His idea of change for the Church was mainly to bring corruption to an end; nor was it the fact that he stubbornly rejected the

Pope's advances: he just did not have the protection of a prince. He did not become the head of an alternative church. Having lost against the Pope's might, he became just a small hitch in the history of the Church. He is mostly remembered by an inscription that marks the place of his execution at the Piazza della Signoria in Florence.

A few years later, Martin Luther, another smart monk with similar ideas about corruption in Rome, also a result of Renaissance ideas (and maybe earlier ones), had a very different fate. He was fortunate enough to live far from Rome and to have learnt from Savonarola's experience that he needed to count with the stable protection of a person like the Elector. Frederick the Wise would actually save him from the wrath of the Church of Rome.

MARTIN LUTHER AND THE
INDIVIDUAL

*I*n 1517, Martin Luther, an Augustinian friar, sent a paper to the Archbishop of Mainz, and it is said he also posted 95 theses on the doors of the church in Wittenberg, where he lived. The theses disputed the claim that indulgences could be bought with money. Later on, in 1521, he refused to retract all of his writings as requested by Pope Leo X and Charles V at the Diet of Worms. Eventually, the Pope excommunicated Luther, and Charles V, the Holy Roman Emperor, declared him an outlaw.

Luther claimed that individual salvation had nothing to do with good deeds, but that it was received only from God's grace through Jesus Christ. He challenged the authority of the Pope and taught that the Bible was the only way to receive knowledge revealed by God. The individual had a direct line to God.

Originally, the only thing in Luther's mind, pretty much like in Savonarola's mind, was to end the corruption that was rotting the core of the Church. Pope Leo, however, was not in the mood to listen to a rebel monk.

According to an article by Bernard Keane, Crikey Politics Editor, of October 2017: *"The immediate concerns of Luther's 95 theses and their link to one of Luther's key doctrinal divergences from the Catholic Church, justification (or salvation) by faith alone, are less important than the core idea that emerged in Protestantism, one that has fundamentally shaped the West ever since: individualism."*

Eric Metaxas, author of *Martin Luther: The man who rediscovered God and changed the world*, totally concurs with that idea: in an article of 30 October, 2017, he asserts: *"For example, the quintessentially modern idea of the individual and of one's personal responsibility before one's self and God rather than before any institution, whether church or state, was as unthinkable before Luther as is color in a world of black and white; and the similarly modern idea of 'the people,' along with the democratic impulse that proceeds from it, was created or at least given a voice by Luther too."* The general consensus appears to be that the Individual began with Luther. I find it extraordinary.

Individualism, that thoroughly Western concept, may have been reinforced by the Reformation, but it would not have prospered in a religion like Islam, for instance. Individualism was a Greek concept fostered by St Paul and introduced through his interpretation of the Book of Genesis. Christianity always was and always remained an individualistic, solipsistic, religion in all of its denominations. After all, the main aim of the Christian is to save his or her own soul. If any other souls are saved, that is great too.

POSSIBLE CHANGES IN
CHRISTIANITY

Pope Francis recently said there was a need for a greater mercy for divorced and remarried Catholics. He proposed a "deeper theology" in terms of the acceptance of women in the Catholic Church. He questioned: "Who am I to judge [gays and gay priests]?". But there is no open acceptance. The Church, a highly conservative institution, doggedly resists change. Some will say that, in any case, the Church remains an anachronism. True. Changes are accepted very slowly. But what the Pope said gives us an idea that doctrinal Christianity is reacting to the perception Western society has of it. Maybe it is too little too late. In any case, as we said, moral values remain stronger in secular society than in all Christian Churches.

Cupitt proposes: *"The Church clings to its old inefficiencies, discriminations and injustices, and repeatedly demands for itself opt-outs from legislation that would require it to get its treatment of its own employees, women, gays and other groups, up to decent contemporary standards. But by its foot-dragging in these matters the Church demonstrates that its version of Christianity is now obsolete. We should leave it, and instead commit ourselves with full religious seriousness to the best of our contemporary secular cultural life. We'll find the air a great deal more wholesome – and more Christian."* [1]

Globalisation is affecting domestic economies and international trade. In the same fashion, overpopulation and mass migrations affect animal species and the environment, and result in frictions among cultures and faiths. The world's cultures (and their religions) are positioning themselves. More changes are coming. No doubt, globalisation is bringing about changes in institutions and values.

If we look at the bigger picture, it is possible to see the common denominator among several phenomena. Why massive migrations to Western Europe, the United States, Canada, Australia, i.e., the most advanced countries? Because there are too many human beings on this Earth, and because it is possible. People move because they have the information and the technology to do it. Human masses are like water. They will seek their own level. You cannot have a rich economy next to a poor one without people moving from one place to the other. It's that simple.

Many institutions are being be affected. The sovereign state is one of them. But also ethnicity, sexuality, marriage, culture, art, language, religion, the sanctity of human life. All of these are changing. They are evolving according to the needs of humankind. These changes are unstoppable and they will proceed at their own pace. Secular Christianity is absorbing those changes. Whether doctrinal Christianity is prepared to catch up with them is a different matter. It remains to be seen.

SCIENTISM

"What we cannot speak about we must pass over in silence"

– **Ludwig Wittgenstein** *(Tractatus-Logico-Philosophicus)*

There is a clear difference between science and scientism. Science occupies itself in obtaining exact and reasoned knowledge of certain objects or facts of the universe. Scientism is characterised by blind faith in science and by its attempts to explain the non-existence of God through science. It has not succeeded thus far.

Many scientists, it would seem, find the concept of religion difficult to accept. Why does religion exist if we are all rational beings? Well, it is all about understanding human behaviour, which is not always rational. Human behaviour, like language, is not always rational. Human behaviour, like language, cannot be reduced to formulas. Religion represents the expression of a human need.

Raymond, the autistic savant in the movie *Rain Man* can work out which cards are left in a stack of several packs. However, he cannot understand the humour in Abbott and Costello's "Who's on first...?" routine. He knows it by heart, but cannot understand it. This may be an extreme example, but having an extraordinary mind does not always mean being able to comprehend human behaviour; or humour, for that matter.

Vattimo argues that the phenomena that are most important to humans are not even considered by science: *"No longer can we assert that since science knows nothing of God, God does not exist. Science isn't even able to establish if it means anything to say that I am in love. All the essential things that characterize our lives, like feelings, values, hope, are not objects of science"* [1]

The limits of science as a system of knowledge are fairly obvious. In science, the truth has to be objective and absolute. In general, things for scientists are binary. True or not true. What scientists find difficult to understand is that the facts are only one side of the picture. Until recently, only artists, and sometimes philosophers, could imagine that something might exist and not exist at the same time. Then, a rare genius came up with a concept like relativity. Nowadays, quantum physicists accept that there may be more than one truth. Objectivity may be non-objectivity.

In general, Western science and philosophy have rejected the inclusiveness of the observer. In order to be able to imagine objective reality, human consciousness is considered separate from the universe. The West rejected Heraclitus and Eastern philosophy and adopted the concept of a measurable external reality. According to Western understanding, we are observers of the universe. With critical thinking, our culture went for knowledge whereas the East went for wisdom. Suffice it to say that, currently, scientists (all or almost all of them) have their doubts about objective reality.

Erich Fromm summarises the concepts that underlie European thought:

"Since Aristotle, the Western world has followed the logical principles of Aristotelian philosophy. This logic is based on the law of identity which states that A is A, the law of contradiction (A is not non-A) and the law of the excluded middle (A cannot be A and non-A, neither A nor non-A)." [2]

Even though I have nothing but appreciation and praise for scientists and their role in the advancement of humanity, it seems to me that scientism has a distorted idea of what science's real function is and of how the opinion of scientists should be valued. Richard Dawkins describes Voltaire's and Thomas Paine's God – the God of the Deists – as a major scientific force:

" ...The deist god is a physicist to end all physics, the alpha and omega of mathematicians, the apotheosis of designers; a hyper-engineer who set up the laws and constants of the universe, fine-tuned them with exquisite precision and foreknowledge, detonated what we would call now the hot big bang, retired and was never heard from again ." [3]

Dawkins will accept one God to some extent, and that is the God of the physicists. There is this hierarchy in his mind whereby physicists understand the concept of God better than other humans: Example: *"The metaphorical or pantheistic <u>God of the physicists is light years away</u> from the interventionist, miracle-wreaking, thought-reading, sin-punishing, prayer-answering God of the Bible, of priests, mullahs and rabbis, and of ordinary language. Deliberately to confuse the two is, in my opinion, an act of intellec-*

tual high treason." ⁴ The only problem with that is that any current possible notion of a God we may have in the West has evolved from Yahweh, the deity we inherited from ancient Judaism. Agreed, Voltaire's God is not a personal god like Yahweh and He is not interested in your sins. But there is no intellectual high treason. Trying to surgically excise the past from Western monotheistic tradition is like saying that the ceiling of the Sistine Chapel, for instance, should not exist because it was painted in the sixteenth century.

Perhaps we should imagine the God of the deists as the creator of the universe. Nothing else. He is not concerned with human beings. Humans do not have to pray to Him. Humans do not have to ask for favours. It is difficult not to like the God of the deists. Even after the Higgs Boson, there is always the doubt Hobbes would have said as to who was the first to create something.

Bertrand Russell explained at one point that, in terms of origin, he could choose between the world and God. And he chose the world. That was a matter of personal opinion, of course.

Alain de Botton, another philosopher, tries to explain the futility of proselytising from an atheistic point of view: *"Attempting to prove the non-existence of God can be an entertaining activity for atheists. Tough-minded critics of religion have found much pleasure in laying bare the idiocy of believers in remorseless detail, finishing only when they felt they had shown up their enemies as thorough-going simpletons or maniacs.*

Though this exercise has its satisfactions, the real issue is not whether God exists or not, but where to take the argument once one decides that he evidently doesn't." ⁵

Scientists solve problems following specific rules. Philosophers approach the larger questions in a completely different way. Søren Kierkegaard explained that the contradictory nature of the coexistence of the universe and the human mind causes the absurd.

Trying to explain the universe in a rational manner is absurd, even if science keeps on trying. Religion seems absurd to the scientist because it provides an explanation to the existence of the universe. The conundrum is that the religious explanation is not a rational one, because that would be absurd. Wittgenstein who, apart from a philosopher was also a mathematician and an engineer, thought along similar lines. And so did Fromm, if we understand how he explained monotheism:

"Following the maturing idea of monotheism in its further consequences can lead only to one conclusion: not to mention God's name at all, not to speak about God. Then God becomes what he potentially is in monotheistic theology, the nameless One, an inexpressible stammer, referring to the unity underlying the phenomenal universe, the ground of all existence; God becomes truth, love, justice. God is I, inasmuch as I am human." [6]

Again, people like Fromm, Wright and Cupitt propose a God that, not being anthropocentric, is expressed in humanity. A God that we cannot talk about. In a way, He has evolved dramatically but, somehow, there are many similarities that connect Him with His predecessor, the ineffable God of the Jews.

A.C. Grayling, a philosopher and an atheist, explains the 'duality' religion/science (adding philosophy to the mix) in adversarial terms: *"Whatever else one might think about the chequered history of the relation between religion and science, at least one thing is clear: that they do indeed compete for the truth about the origin of the universe, the nature of human beings, and whether the universe manifests evidence of intelligent design. Religion also competes with secular philosophy over the question of the foundations of morality and whether the existence of the universe and humanity serves a purpose set by a supernatural agency, or whether the making of moral meaning is the responsibility of human beings themselves."* [7]

In terms of Judaism and Christianity, I believe the religion/science 'duality' is not quite what as black and white as it seems to Grayling. There are common points that should be explored. And there is a historic connection that cannot be ignored. Moreover, the etymology of 'morality' bases the word on 'mores maiorum' the customs or habits of our elders. How does Christianity compete with secular philosophy in that respect? As long as we respect what our ancestors did, we are moral individuals. That is, we are responsible for our morals. As far as I know, Christianity is happy with that. What Grayling states as to whether the existence of the universe and humanity serves a divine purpose appears to be an over-simplification of the issue. Not all schools of Western secular philosophy deny the possibility of a purpose. Being secular, of course, it would deny that the purpose is established by a supernatural agency. The assertion is tautological. Without an actor there is no purpose.

I have chosen to believe in the possibility of the existence of a deist God that, from my perspective, is the one that evolved from the God of Judaism, Yahweh, the one that was cruel and jealous, and so on, when he was a tribal god. Yes. I cannot believe in the pre-existence of Jesus or in his divinity. Jesus was an extraordinary man. But I share with Wright the notion that, if God exists, He has evolved with us. In this day and age He should perhaps not be the Creator of the Universe, but He should be perfect and accepting. Why do I choose the God of the Jews above all others? Because I am an agnostic Christian. Yes, maybe that is paradoxical. But that is the way I feel. I was brought up a Catholic but never quite believed. However, all the images that make me feel comfortable are those of that God. Christianity inherited that God. And if there is a God, *that* is the image I carry with me. If you are a monotheist, that God should be your God too, because Judaism and Islam also start with Him. You can call Him God, Yahweh, El, or Allah, or choose not to name him at all. I am not going to judge you and I expect you, religious or atheist, not to judge me either.

WELL, Dawkins has a few things to say about the God of the Jews, and none of them are good:

"The God of the Old Testament is arguably the most unpleasant character in all fiction: jealous and proud of it; a petty, unjust, unforgiving control-freak; a vindictive, bloodthirsty ethnic cleanser, a misogynistic, homophobic, racist, infanticidal, genocidal, filicidal, pestilential, megalomaniacal, sadomasochistic, capriciously malevolent bully." [8]

He doesn't seem to be holding any punches. But has he understood the Old Testament? Well, is it possible to defend God against any of the accusations Professor Dawkins is hurling at Him? No. It isn't possible... that is, if we apply his rules, but the game he proposes is a very unfair game. The Old Testament God is a tribal god who has to defend his tribe at any cost.

If I took any book on witchcraft or black magic or alchemy or astrology and quoted from it, I would be able to say that science is pure superstition, that there is nothing rational about it. And science has evolved from all those primitive disciplines, only that it has developed as human knowledge has grown. Any scientist can complain about the animal sacrifices made by priests in the Temple of Jerusalem. And I could say that, to this day, laboratories sacrifice mice and monkeys and apes, and all kinds of other animals, in the interest of science. I could say that science creates weapons that kill people. It created the bombs that went down on Hiroshima and Nagasaki. I could also say that Nazi scientists performed vivisections on human beings, again, in the interest of science. Human beings can use both, science and religion, for their own evil purposes.

What is also evident in this argument is that it is possible to take anything out of context. The notion of God has evolved, and is evolving, with humanity. Three or four thousand years ago, God was perceived by a tribe of illiterate shepherds in a way that is no longer compatible with the perception we may have of Him nowadays.

When asked about the Answer to the Ultimate Question of Life, The Universe, and Everything, the computer in *The hitchhiker's guide to the galaxy* took 7½ million years to find out that it was 42. Was Douglas just being funny or was he sending a message to scientists and rationalists?

I cannot remember who said that trying to explain religion in terms of science is like trying to describe the "Mona Lisa" in terms of pigments. Maybe nobody did and I just imagined it. In any case, I think it is a great metaphor.

Among recent authors, Craig A James, an engineer, applied the notion of memes and memetics to religion. He explored the idea that religion is like a virus and that it replicated itself. In his book *The religious virus* he took the concept to extremes:

"*...With our new understanding of evolution and memes, we looked at religion's evolution from the time of Jesus to present day, and studied several more memes that evolved in the Religion Virus memeplex, including a further refinement of intolerance, how guilt was turned to a major force of persuasion, the heaven/hell memes, and how St Paul expanded Yahweh to become the god of gentiles. We also looked at the important concept of synergy, how the heaven/hell, guilt, monotheism and intolerance memes work together.*" [9] Wow! A scientific analysis. What can I say?

Dawkins himself applies the 'meme' principle to religion in *The god delusion*:

"*The fact that religion is ubiquitous probably means that it has worked to the benefit of something, but it may not be us or our genes. It may be to the benefit of only the religious ideas themselves, to the extent that they behave in a somewhat gene-like way, as replicators.*" [10]

Absurd? Both James and Dawkins explain the existence of religion by means of the existence of religion. Well, I don't want to get philosophical about it. I'm just glad Dawkins didn't devote the whole book to it. Trying to resolve a question that pertains to the humanities requires methods that are applicable to the humanities. The 'meme', that pseudo humanistic idea posited by Dawkins in *The selfish gene*, is a concept that appears to allow for one such method. However, if we apply a scientific method to a question concerning the humanities we will certainly come up with an absurd answer.

Openly mixing and matching science and religion results in even more bizarre concepts. Creationists in America have introduced the notion that 'intelligent design' has to be taught in science classes. Most people would agree that this is a preposterous idea. It is the flip side of what we have been discussing. 'Intelligent design' is the negation of evolution and science. It does not make sense. It wants to provide a scientific answer to God. There is no such thing.

These are the extremes. The lunatic fringe who speak in tongues and handle serpents versus the Darwinian evolutionists who expect us to explain God in terms of science. Should there be other positions? As I mentioned before, Robert Wright (*Nonzero, The evolution of god*) appears to have a teleological answer to the conundrum. Something that could be described as a supercharged turbo Holy Spirit: whatever our aim is, that aim *is* God.

There is a more complex concept: the parallel direction of evolution and religion. Is there an aim in evolution? Evolution does not appear to have any ultimate goal, like Christianity has. However, the result of the way in which we evolve is that we adapt to the conditions in which we live and life becomes easier. Life has become easier. And we have survived thus far. Organised Christianity, only preoccupied with humans, aims at spiritual perfection. A dangerous goal. So does Islam, from a totally different perspective.

How does religion perpetuate itself? The answer is simple and it has to do with feelings. There is no meme (please!). There is no virus. Why does a Catholic feel calm and contented when she is in a Catholic church? Why do I feel at home there if I am not even certain about believing in God? It is simple: my parents taught me the principles of the Catholic faith. They showed me with their example. They also sent me to Catholic school. Maybe that was wrong, but I am sure my parents wanted only the best for me. That is how religion persists, or at least that is how it has persisted thus far. It is meant to be a good thing. One respects one's parents. One abides by the rules. One grows up within a culture. It is as simple as that.

St Augustine would have agreed: your parents guide you towards your religion:

"Nevertheless I utterly refused to entrust the healing of the maladies of my soul to these philosophers, because they ignored the saving name of Christ. I therefore decided to remain a catechumen in the Catholic Church, which was what my parents wanted, at least until I could clearly see a light to guide my steps." [11]

It is also very easy, for instance, for somebody who is born within a certain faith, to consider the other cultures as "not the true one". You are taught that the rest are wrong and you are right. The Catholic Church is the true faith because it continued where the Jews stopped. And it stayed its course when Protestants left the right path following false prophets. Martin Luther, Calvin, Zwingli. And let's not talk about Henry VIII who, of course, will burn in hell forever.

Tom Holland tells us an anecdote to do with Dawkins who, much to his chagrin, had to accept some Christianity within himself: *"On 16 July 2018, one of the world's best-known scientists, a man as celebrated for his polemics against religion as for his writings on evolutionary biology, sat listening to the bells of an English cathedral. 'So much nicer than the aggressive-sounding 'Allahu-Akhbar', Richard Dawkins tweeted 'Or is that just my cultural upbringing?'"* [12]

As with everything else, there is also a reason for that. We have an atavistic need to belong. Reza Aslan said: *"I began to rethink the faith and culture of my forefathers, finding in them a deeper, more intimate familiarity than I ever had as a child, the kind that comes from reconnecting with an old friend after many years apart*". He went back to his religion. Understanding what he did is easy. The faith of your elders gives you that warm, fuzzy feeling that no amount of atheistic reasoning can give you. In Islam, if you want to believe, you have to go all the way. There is no middle ground. In the case of Christianity, the West has also evolved in principles that pervade our secular culture, and it is quite acceptable to be a Christian agnostic, as we have seen.

There is another, more critical explanation, which Grayling summarises very well: *"To put matters at their simplest, the major reason for the continuance of religious belief in a world which might otherwise have long moved beyond it, is indoctrination of children before they reach the age of reason, together with all or some combination of social pressure to conform, social reinforcement of religious institutions and traditions, emotion, and (it has to be said) ignorance—of science, of psychology, of history in general and of the history and actual doctrines of religions themselves"* [13]. This, of course, ignores the fact that children grow up, acquire reason, and are free to choose whether to remain within a religion or move away from it. What remains, as I said, is that warm, fuzzy, feeling that stays with you the rest of your life.

Historically, religions perpetuated themselves in ways that are not acceptable any more. In many Muslim countries the sins of apostasy and Christian proselytism still carry the death penalty. In Catholic Church dogma apostates were assigned one of the lowest rungs in Hell and, of course, until the seventeenth century they were burnt at the stake. Jews also shunned and often stoned apostates.

By the same token, any rational person with an Aristotelian formation will find that labelling religion as a bunch of lies is a very easy thing to do. Religion takes very little to disprove applying common sense, or from a scientific point of view. It only takes one articulate atheist. And many of them are very articulate. But does it take you anywhere?

The question of God, as opposed to the question of religion, is a different matter. Dawkins sometimes comes up with infantile riddles of the kind we used to ask in primary school: *"The whole argument turns on the familiar question 'Who made God', which most thinking people discover for themselves. A designer God cannot be used to explain organized complexity because any God capable of designing anything would have to be complex enough to demand the same kind of explanation in his own right. God presents an infinite regress from which he cannot help us to escape."* [14] The conundrum lies in trying to understand a concept like God, or the universe for that matter, with a human mind. The answer is absurd: turtles all the way down.

Wisely– perhaps I should say also humbly– de Botton explains the usefulness of science from a different perspective: *"Science should matter to us not only because it helps us to control parts of the world, but also because it shows us things that we will never master. Thus we would do well to meditate daily, rather as the religious do on their God, on the 9.5 trillion kilometres which comprise a single light year, or perhaps on the luminosity of the largest known star in our galaxy, Eta Carinae, 7,500 light years distant, 400 times the size of the sun and 4 million times as bright."* [15]

The scientific research conducted in the second half of the 19th century by Darwin and other scientists was never meant to disprove the existence of God. It ended up disproving St Paul's Christian interpretation of the *Tanach*.

DARWIN AND THE EVOLUTION OF THE SPECIES

With his book *On the origin of the species*, Charles Darwin gave form to a theory that his illustrious grandfather, Dr Erasmus Darwin, among others, had pre announced in the eighteenth century. The idea had been in people's minds for some time. Species evolve. The human species is part of that evolution. Dr Darwin appears to have suspected it:

"Just as with the fossils in the Derbyshire caves, it was clear – although Linnaeus dogmatically clung to the contrary view – that some species had vanished over time, new ones had emerged, and older types had mutated." [1]

A few years before the birth of Jesus, Lucretius had ideas that could be considered very similar to evolutionism. The Comte de Buffon was preeminent among the naturalists who foresaw the evolution of the species, especially the relationship of man to other apes:

"And, if it be once admitted that there are families among plants and animals, that the ass belongs to the family of the horse, and differs from him only by degeneration; with equal propriety may it be concluded, that the monkey belongs to the family of man; that the monkey is a man degenerated; that man and the monkey have sprung from a common stock, like the horse and ass; that each family, either among animals or vegetables, has been derived from the same origin and even that all animated beings have proceeded from a single species, which, in the course of ages, has produced, by improving and degenerating, all the different races that now exist." [2]

Charles Darwin researched and published very detailed evidence that what Buffon and his grandfather had predicted was unequivocally true. To many, especially to Bible-obsessed Anglicans, that pill was very hard to swallow. There was widespread reaction from various other religious sectors as well. The book and the theory themselves do not include any atheistic declarations. It is just that the concept of evolution, as expressed by authors like Lucretius, had been abandoned for so long, and the Bible had been taken literally for so long, that this reminder that humans are descended from apes was not easy to accept.

Stephen Greenblatt, in *"The rise and fall of Adam and Eve"* discusses Darwin's theory in these terms: *"Darwinism is not incompatible with belief in God, but it is certainly incompatible with belief in Adam and Eve. Nothing in The Descent of Man, published in 1871, allowed for even the remotest possibility that our species originated in the form of two exemplary, fresh-minted humans at home in a paradisal garden. Darwin had already made public his evolutionary theory in his 1859, The Origin of Species. Written for non specialists, the book had had an enormous impact, but it had deliberately left humans out of the enormous range of species it discussed"*. [3] The problem with this is that the two blond,

European-looking humans were definitely a Christian interpretation. Had Professor Greenblatt specified *"with <u>Christian belief in Adam and Eve</u>"*, I would have agreed. And it is true, Darwinism does not allow for the possibility of two *'exemplary, fresh-minted'* humans, but that is not what the original Jewish myth says. As we shall see, in all probability, the Torah was proto-Darwinian and therefore more than compatible with evolution. The separation of humans from animals was introduced at a much later date, by St Paul.

A nineteenth-century Victorian Englishman, Darwin himself was not the totally materialistic, atheistic naturalist his admirers claim him to be. It is a well-known fact that Darwin's wife who was also his cousin Emma Wedgewood, was a devout Christian, as was his extended family, and that she exerted some influence on the way he phrased his book. The last paragraph of *Origin of the species* has two versions. In the first one he did not include a mention of God. In the second version, which appeared from the second to the sixth editions, he added "by the Creator". Many people say that this was to appease his wife and family, and the public in general. He also mentioned this amendment later in his life and was clearly unhappy to have introduced it. The paragraph reads:

"This, from the war of nature, from famine and death, the most exalted object which we are capable of conceiving, namely the production of the higher animals, directly follows. There is grandeur in this view of life, with its several powers, having been originally breathed by the Creator into a few forms or into one; and that, whilst this planet has gone circling on according to the fixed law of gravity, from so simple a beginning endless forms most beautiful and most wonderful have been, and are being evolved." [4]

Notice the word *"breathed"*, which was left in the editions that do not mention God. It is a biblical word. Living in nineteenth century England, it is quite probable that, for all his materialistic assertions, Darwin was really an agnostic.

Stories about Darwin's death appear to confirm the fact that he was an agnostic.

It was almost midnight that Wednesday, 19 April 1882. The big house was located in the best area of the village of Downe, some sixteen miles from the city of London. In the master bedroom there two or three people surrounding the old man, who was very sick. He woke up. He was very dizzy. Very confused. Henrietta took his hand. The convulsions and vomits started again. From his pale lips came a tired exclamation: "Oh, my Lord", and again: "Oh, my Lord". That moment he almost passed out. Henrietta gave him some aromatic salts.

"Where's mum?" he asked, a little upset.

When he was told that Emma was resting, he said he was glad and attempted a smile, while telling two of the girls in the room with him that they were the best nurses in the world. They all knew he was in a lot of pain.

When they called his wife, the old man felt he was going to pass out. SheEmma took his hand and gave him a bit of whisky to alleviate him, but the pain was unbearable. By the time the doctors arrived, he had totally lost consciousness. Everyone present knew there was no more hope. That is the way Charles Robert Darwin died". That is more or less the way Adrian Desmond and James Moore describe the scene in *"Darwin"*, their excellent biography dated 1991.

He was buried in Westminster Abbey. Had he been an atheist he could have made provisions for that not to happen. Even his atheist admirers cannot deny that fact. Darwin is buried in the house of God.

Evolutionism had commenced before Darwin, but something very innovative Darwin contributed to it was the idea of natural selection, i.e. *"the survival of the fittest"*, of the strongest. In that respect, Christianity would appear exactly the opposite. Jesus Christ had taught compassion for the weak, the poor, the sick. His life, and his death, teach exactly that. Our society has upheld those principles. Darwin was concerned about the lack of cohesion between his theories and Western morals and ethics. In her book *"Darwin, social darwinism and eugenics"*, Diane B Paul quotes him saying *"... natural selection has not contributed anything to our modern civilisation..."*. Although he agreed with those Christian principles, his idea was that, if society treated them as something central and important it would run the risk of degenerating and decaying.

Western and Christian societies, i.e., liberal democracies, nowadays respect and protect the weakest, even outside of their areas of influence, although at the same time they promote competition. Those who are most apt are the ones that triumph within those societies. But the weak, as well as the strong, benefit from evolution.

Tom Holland successfully summarises the differences between darwinism and Christianity: *"To believe that God had become man and suffered the death of a slave was to believe that there might be strength in weakness, and victory in defeat. Darwin's theory, more radically than anything that previously had emerged from Christian civilisation, challenged that assumption. Weakness was nothing to be valued."*... *"For eighteen long centuries, the Christian conviction that all human life was sacred had been underpinned by one doctrine more than any other: that man and woman had been created in God's image. The divine was to be found as much in the pauper, the convict or in the prostitute as it was in the gentleman with his private income and book-lined study".* [5]

How is that science, a product of the West, supports evolutionism, natural selection and darwinism in general but Western societies behave abiding by other principles? As we were saying, Western societies of the twenty-first century have a very clear idea of what is right and what is wrong. That is based on something. The idea that suffering is more decent than making suffer is the one that has triumphed in the West. The 'strength' of renouncing to something because of a worthy cause is respected without calling 'weak' the person who does that. Those certainties are part of a legacy that we received more than twenty centuries ago, ideas that in those days were revolutionary and transformed the world. Clearly, our current convictions are convictions based on Christian morals and ethics. In that respect, Darwin's fears concerning weakness in the West were unfounded. He was wrong. Even having appeared in the Christian West, science, partially-derived from Western culture, an activity devoted solely to the rational aspect of our lives has not yet understood the way our culture operates.

Maybe science, that human creation, will never totally comprehend what Adam and Eve understood after having eaten the fruit of the Tree of Knowledge of Good and Evil.

AGNOSTICISM

There are some middle-of-the-road, agnostic authors, like Robert Wright who, without totally accepting the existence of God, proclaim there is an impetus and a direction in our biological and cultural evolution that may be indicative of a deity. We are going somewhere. And, indeed, things appear to be improving for our species. We have progressed.

Maybe the purpose of our life is just to be happy and enjoy it. Maybe there is real wisdom in the Ecclesiastes.

By agreeing with Wright, I find myself in the most despised (by both theists and their opponents) of all positions within the spectrum of the theist-atheist argument: the agnostic. Dawkins, for instance, loathes agnostics. He even agrees with an agnostic-hating preacher he remembers from his childhood:

"... What this preacher couldn't stand was agnostics: namby-pamby, mushy pap, weak-tea, weedy, pallid fence-sitters. He was partly right, but for wholly the wrong reason." [1]

Nowadays, even mentioning the possibility of God among educated people is a recipe for disaster. Wright explains the predicament of the agnostic:

"... And maybe the source of this higher purpose, the source of the moral order, is something that qualifies for the label 'god' in at least some sense of that word.

The previous sentence is hardly a fervent expression of religious faith: in fact, it's essentially agnostic. Even so, I don't recommend uttering it at, say, an Ivy League faculty gathering unless you want people to look at you as if you'd started speaking in tongues. In modern intellectual circles, speculating seriously about God's existence isn't a path to widespread esteem." [2]

Agnostics, myself included are literally 'those who do not know'. It is good, however, to find oneself in the company of people like Charles Darwin and some of the best philosophers in history. Thomas Huxley, also an agnostic, reflects:

"The one thing in which most of these good people agreed was the one thing in which I differed from them. They were quite sure they had attained a certain 'gnosis' – had, more or less successfully, solved the problem of existence; while I was quite sure I had not, and had a pretty strong conviction that the problem was insoluble. And, with Hume and Kant on my side, I could not think myself presumptuous in holding fast by that opinion..." [3]

I cannot but envy those who are so sure of their beliefs, be they atheists or theists. It is the sort of conviction required to be a suicide bomber.

Anti-theistic authors, like Christopher Hitchens (and countless more) claim that the concept of God has done nothing but damage to the species and that we are going to be much better off the moment we renounce religion altogether. A tempting thought for some in view of the spread of Islamic terrorism, among other curses we have to endure this century.

Hitchens was never one to mince his words:

"If I cannot definitively prove that the usefulness of religion is in the past, and that its foundational books are transparent fables, and that it is a man-made imposition, and that it has been an enemy of science and inquiry, and that it has subsisted largely on lies and fears, and been the accomplice of ignorance and guilt as well as of slavery, genocide, racism, and tyranny, I can most certainly claim that religion is now fully aware of these criticisms." [4]

No doubt, doctrinal religion is man-made. It is the body of rites and regulations some men have come up with for the rest of humanity to communicate with their god. It has served that purpose for thousands of years. And it is still useful to billions of people. Reza Aslan describes it as a language: *"Beyond the myths and rituals, the temples and cathedrals, the dos and don'ts that have, for millennia, separated humanity into different and often competing camps of belief, religion is little more than a 'language' made up of symbols and metaphors that allows believers to communicate, to one another and to themselves, the ineffable experience of faith."* [5]

Hitchens appears to have seen these issues in black and white, like many atheists. Discussing myths, Stephen Greenblatt explains the nuances: *"I have been fascinated throughout my life by the stories that we humans invent in an attempt to make sense of our existence, and I have come to understand that the term 'lie' is a woefully inadequate description of either the motive or the content of these stories, even at their most fantastical."* [6]

In any case, much of the problem Hitchens mentions is related to the Church's interpretation of Hebrew Scripture. The Hebrew Bible, or *Tanakh*, as we shall see, is a collection of oral traditions and stories that explain the prehistory of the Jewish nation. Its stories are not 'transparent fables'. They were oral history that became scripture, traditions that were transmitted from generation to generation since time immemorial. Human beings relate past events and, as part of history, those events become stories. Greenblatt, again: *"Humans cannot live without stories. We surround ourselves with them; make the up in our sleep; we tell them to our children; we pay to have them told to us. Some of us create them professionally. And a few of us, myself included, spend our entire lives trying to understand their beauty, power, and influence."* [7]

Without trying to defend doctrinal Christianity, the other charges Hitchens hurls at religion may be applicable to any institution that has lasted several thousand years and there are not many. Democracy in its infancy did not include slaves, foreigners or women. Actually, women were excluded until very recently. Foreigners are still excluded. Democracy is as exclusive as the sovereign state. Proposing to discard democracy on account of its past mistakes would sound like an absurd proposition to me.

Yes, the beliefs of the civilised world have already changed. Christianity and Western culture appear to be one and the same, a continuum with different gradations of religiosity. Going back to democracy, we must remember that racial segregation, for instance, was a reality until very recently in advanced countries like the United States, South Africa and

Australia. There were times when democracy was not synonymous with liberalism. The same principle applies to the Church. If it wants to survive it will have to accept the realities of the 21st century. In any case, as we posit here, Christianity has definitely survived outside the Church. The wide acceptance of same-sex marriage in the West, for instance, is proof of that.

Maybe some 'miracle' will bring the Church in line with current secular Christianity and Western culture.

Robert Wright is always optimistic:

"Maybe, in the end, a mercilessly scientific account of our predicament... is actually compatible with a truly religious worldview and is part of the process that refines a religious worldview, moving it closer to truth.

These two big 'clash' questions can be put into one sentence: Can religions in the modern world reconcile themselves to one another, and can they reconcile themselves to science? I think their history points to affirmative answers" [8]

What Wright says is one of the points of this book. Christianity has undergone change and must undergo more change. There is no escape from that. Christianity now survives in the West as a set of ethical and moral principles we have inherited from Jesus Christ. The Catholic and Protestant Churches are slowly accepting that theirs is a secondary role.

The Western atheists' reaction to the notion of God probably originates in the profound disappointment we all have with organised religion. The lies and scandals have been many. Popes had concubines and children. Popes appointed their own sons as cardinals. Luther was a rabid anti-semite, as was Calvin to a lesser degree. Henry VIII created the Church of

England because the Pope would not annul his marriage to Catherine of Aragon. During World War II, Pius XII almost sided with the Nazis. This century, cardinals enriched themselves and built private palaces with Church funds. Paedophile priests ruined the lives of many girls and boys. An Australian Cardinal, George Pell, was convicted of sexually abusing two choir boys in Melbourne Cathedral, although the Supreme Court acquitted him one year later because the evidence was inconclusive. The Banco Ambrosiano, whose main shareholder was the Vatican Bank, was connected to fraud and crime some years ago. And so on. The scandal has never stopped.

Apart from the priests, the rites, and the dogma of the Church, Christianity continues, unfazed, embedded in the greatest civilisation ever.

Paradoxically, Charles Darwin appears to have wanted to believe in the God of Christianity but found it difficult in view of his discoveries concerning evolution.

Sometimes our hearts point in a certain direction but our minds say no. Very often, however, the questions and the answers cannot be as simple as yes or no. In my life I have discovered that it is possible, even for an agnostic, to connect spectacularly with God every now and then; to find oneself in awe of the relationship between humans and their God. It happens when you approach Bernini's Baldacchino, the monumental canopy on twisted Solomonic pillars that covers the main altar in St Peter's Basilica. Hagia Sophia, in Constantinople (now Istanbul), is probably as close you can get to God on Earth. Built in the sixth century AD, it exemplifies the glory that was Byzantine architecture. Any impression a current building or skyscraper can give you, regardless of its size, is dwarfed in comparison. Only the love of God could create the grandeur you see in Hagia Sophia. Even if you are a religious skeptic and have your doubts, it becomes clear that no amount of rational analysis can explain the power of that connection with the Divine. Of course, these are things that prove nothing in terms of the existence of God. Keeping our minds open doesn't hurt, I suppose.

It is quite possible, as we were saying, that the resurgence of atheism is just a reaction to the problems we have had with organised religion, basically with the Christian churches, with their concocted doctrines and with the personalities of their leaders. History, however, has no 'reset' button. We cannot erase what has happened. The only thing we can do is assume it. Ditching the concept of God altogether because of the dishonesty involved in the history of Christianity would be like throwing the baby with the bathwater.

Trying to find what is salvageable, Alain de Botton attempts to reconcile our current needs with religion: *"One can be left cold by the doctrines of the Christian Trinity and the Buddhist Eightfold Path and yet at the same time be interested in the ways in which religions deliver sermons, promote morality, engender a spirit of community, make use of art and architecture, inspire travels, train minds and encourage gratitude at the beauty of spring. In a world beset by fundamentalists of both believing and secular varieties, it must be possible to balance a rejection of religious faith with a selective reverence for religious rituals and concepts."* [9]

Americans are finding that accepting their history is a difficult proposition. The flag of some Southern States, a symbol of slavery and oppression, together with the monuments to secessionist Generals like Lee and Stonewall Jackson have been removed from view. The reaction is a logical one, but just hiding those symbols will not make them disappear altogether. The existence of Nazi Germany in the 1930s and the horrible things that human beings have done to each other cannot and should not be erased from our collective memory. The idea should be rather learning from the experience. In the case of Christianity, we know that there has been deception. Denying it is as naive as having believed it. Actually, the big lie would be ignoring our past. Maybe, some time in the future, the Churches of the West will participate in the quest for a solution. Is it likely? Perhaps not likely, but possible.

As we have been saying, the whole of Europe, basically the whole of our Western culture which we are so proud of, grew out of Christianity. Our names, our most respected art, our toponymy, much of our language, even our holidays (holy days) are constant evidence of that.

We are contradictory creatures who have emerged from animal origins with a dual nature. So, saying we are mere animals is simplifying things to an extent that not even Hitchens would have accepted. The way I see it, our consciousness is a divine gift, if we want to use that word. It is the collective divine in us. What the Church calls the Holy Spirit.

We know that everything is finite, that everything comes to an end, even us; that was one of Adam and Eve's discoveries. We die. Christianity promised us immortality through belief in Jesus Christ. It is quite clear to many of us that there is no such thing. We know that too. But that is all right. Maybe what we need, rather than immortality, is an indication as to the meaning of our extremely brief lives.

But Christianity is not evil, as many atheists argue. That is probably the main fault I can find in Christopher Hitchens book *God is not great: How religion poisons everything*. The theme of evil runs throughout the book (including its title), much to the detriment of its impeccable logic (you ask yourself, why would anybody want to impose this evil on humanity?). You could argue that there have been religious individuals who have historically tricked other individuals for their own benefit. But institutions? Why? How is this evil perpetuated? Are students taught at seminaries and rabbinical schools that what they are going to unleash on people is this horrible lie? Are they taught that this lie is going to keep believers ignorant and ruin their lives? Is that going to be the profession of priests and rabbis? Do they all look and sound and act like bad people? Of course not. Hitchens did not believe, I am sure, that there is malice in Christianity, Judaism or even Islam. He was a clever man. However, he chose to use evil in God as a theme, probably because it made the whole book all the more compelling. Much of his argument was based on seventeenth and eighteenth century Deistic thought. All religious teachers are bad, he said. Perhaps the only exception is the description of his primary school teacher, Mrs Jean Watts, *"a good, sincere, simple woman"*. I am sure she must have been a delightful English lady. Regardless of how brilliant his argument is and how convincing it seems at first sight, the book falters because it becomes an indictment of human society, culture and behaviour as a whole.

Following the theme of fraud, Hitchens affirms without hesitation that:

"Credulity may be a form of innocence, and even innocuous in itself, but it provides a standing invitation for the wicked and the clever to exploit their brothers and sisters, and is thus one of humanity's great vulnerabilities. No honest account of the growth and persistence of

religion, or the reception of miracles and revelations, is possible without reference to this stubborn fact." [10]

This is an obvious exaggeration. It presupposes that all priests, rabbis, mullahs, nuns and monks, religious teachers, and that even includes Mrs Jean Watts, are (or were) hypocrites who expect (or expected) to profit from it. The growth and persistence of religion is not due to a massive conspiracy. Religion persists because it is culturally transmitted. Sure enough, throughout history some charlatans have been involved and have profited from religious groups.

The funny thing, according to Alain de Botton, is that: *"The secular are at this moment in history a great deal more optimistic than the religious – something of an irony, given the frequency with which the latter have been derided by the former for their apparent naivety and credulousness. It is the secular whose longing for perfection has grown so intense as to lead them to imagine that paradise might be realized on this earth after just a few more years of financial growth and medical research. With no evident awareness of the contradiction they may, in the same breath, gruffly dismiss a belief in angels while sincerely trusting that the combined powers of the IMF, the medical research establishment, Silicon Valley and democratic politics could together cure the ills of mankind."* [11]

At one point, Hitchens questions the idea of the religious scam:

"Do the preachers and prophets also believe, or do they too just 'believe in belief'? Do they ever think to themselves, this is too easy? And do they rationalize the trick by saying that either (a) if these wretches weren't listening to me they'd be in even worse shape; or (b) that if it doesn't do them any good then it still can't be doing them much harm?" [12]

However, after all his analysis of general wickedness in religion, he cannot provide an overall answer to any of his doubts:

"The study of religion suggests to me that, while it cannot possibly get along without great fraud and also minor fraud, this remains a fascinating and somewhat open question." [13]

Somewhere along the line within the history of the Judaeo-Christian faith there must have been some deception. Did Moses come down from Mount Sinai with the tablets? Did Yahweh write them with his finger? I would say no (especially because there was no Hebrew writing at that stage), but those tablets, and Moses if he ever existed, provided a good moral code and political guidance to the Hebrews, and to all the Gentiles that followed. Did Saul of Tarsus hear Jesus Christ on the way to Damascus? I would say no, but he provided the seed for the Romans (and the Gentiles in general) to adopt and adapt a form of the Jewish faith that appeared to be more inclusive, and that was useful and positive. And also, paraphrasing Robert Wright, that was the evolution of the illusion that humanity needed at the time.

The original Yahweh was more than just anthropocentric. He was Judaic. Of course he was. He was the notion of God as conceived by men who were Jews. He was the creator of the universe but he was, somehow, exclusive. He had chosen mankind and the Jewish tribes. The God of Christianity is still the creator of the universe. He is not as exclusive in that he accepts anyone who is born into or converts to Christianity (nobody else though); and he is still fiercely anthropocentric. His son is God but he is also a man.

The good aspect of that God originally El, Elohim, Adonai or Yahweh that has come down to us through history is that He is the all-powerful creator of the universe. But He doesn't even need to be the originator. He can be whatever it is in us that takes us where we want to go. He can be a purpose. The teleological God of the West.

In a way, following Nietzsche, *'God is dead'*, but there is no gain in declaring God null and void. And a similar reasoning may be applied Christianity. Our brain has incorporated it together with our culture. Furthermore, we cannot negate it without negating ourselves. Many of us in the West even have biblical names, including Hitchens.

What is strange in Hitchens is that he often objected not to organised religion itself (dogma, which may be where the lies are), but to religious faith:

"There still remain four irreducible objections to religious faith: that it wholly misrepresents the origins of man and the cosmos, that because of this original error it manages to combine the maximum of servility with the maximum of solipsism, that it is both the result and the cause of dangerous sexual repressions, and that it is ultimately grounded on wish-thinking".[14]

Those four points are misleading. There is no error in the monotheistic religions concerning the creation of man and the cosmos. You may or may not believe that God was responsible for the Big Bang. If you're a scientist you will probably prefer the Higgs Boson. The question is, is it a better, more rational, explanation? And this has nothing to do with the supposedly eternal life of our souls. As for the way the Torah presents the creation of humans, we will see that, leaving aside the participation of God in it, it is a pretty accurate and beautiful description of what must have happened from a scientific point of view. The way it has been misinterpreted for a long time is another matter. I will come back to this point.

There is no servility in Christianity. There is love and charity. Love for God and charity towards our fellow human beings. There may be some solipsism in that the wish of every Christian is to be saved. But the counterpart is the existence of the Holy Spirit, the Divinity that we all share.

I discuss sexual repression in another chapter and I believe Higgins refers to it mainly in reference to Islam, as it applies to all Muslims, whereas the main sexual repression in Christianity has to do with clerical celibacy.

No deep analysis of the Judaeo-Christian religious tradition can begin by dismissing the Torah as a bunch of old lies. The concepts I explore here will suggest a reality that does not lend itself to that sort of analysis.

Dismissing God altogether is a gratuitous mirage, an Aristotelian fallacy. Scientifically, God does not exist. No doubt. Nobody knows if He does or doesn't exist. The question is whether, as Wright puts it, having created God, man has proved that there is a purpose, an aim in our acts.

LOSING MY RELIGION: THE IMPACT OF A TV CLIP

The year was 1990 and twenty-nine-year-old Tarsem Singh Dhandwar, an Indian-American final-year student at the Art Center College of Design, was probably selling cars as he used to do to support himself, or maybe doing homework, or resting at home. He didn't have a mobile phone because in those days not many people did. In any case, the phone rang and somebody said that a guy by the name of Stipe wanted to talk to him. An unknown group called R.E.M. needed a video for the first song of their album "Out of time". Stipe had written lyrics for some simple mandolin music composed by the group guitarist, Peter Buck. The song was called "Losing my religion" although, according to Stipe, it had nothing to do with religion and a lot to do with obsession and unrequited love. Apparently, the idiom "to lose one's religion" is a Southern euphemism for "losing it" or "being impolite".

As a result of that phone conversation Tarsem spent one and a half days in Georgia, chatting and hanging out and doing intense collaborative work, and Stipe and Tarsem exchanged ideas on what was expected of the clip. The time the two artists spent together culminated in a brilliant, iconic, video that won several MTV Video Awards and the Grammy for Best Short Form Video.

The music and lyrics were excellent, but what wrapped up the whole product was the visual part of the clip. Tarsem had decided to take the title literally.

The picture gives a sensation of irretrievable loss. A pitcher full of milk tips over from a windowsill and breaks into a thousand pieces. The milk spills all over the floor. There are images borrowed from a story by García Márquez about an old angel that falls from the sky; there is an amazing group of chiaroscuro figures inspired by Caravaggio, and some gay interpretation of Indian deities (the latter, probably Tarsem's cultural contribution). The old angel loses his toupee and everybody laughs, St Sebastian has the arrows stuck with electrical tape. Included among the religious imagery are some stills in the style of Soviet posters. Another lost religion. The picture Tarsem conveyed was one of decay, of pathetic reality, as well as disillusionment and deception. The clip definitely gives the viewer the feeling of a terrible loss. Stipe provided some weird dancing very hip in the nineties and lip-synched the lyrics, with final verses such as "But that was just a dream, try, cry, why, try/ That was just a dream, just a dream, just a dream/ Dream".

According to early estimates, the track could have sold two million copies. It sold ten million. The idea of losing one's religion had literally struck a chord with young listeners in the Western world. In reality, the notion of loss and the actual loss were not as bad as all that. Christianity appears to have remained the essential element of the West.

THE WEST

What is the West? Discussing current phenomena, Don Cupitt provides his idea of what the West is: *"This new West is something like a culmination of human history hitherto, for it is marked by the appearance of the first fully emancipated human beings – people who know themselves to be the only makers of their own world-view, knowledge-systems, technologies and values. Their world is purely human and secular. Their politics is liberal-democratic, their economic order is 'social market' or 'guided capitalist', and their ethic is above all humanitarian. They pay lip-service, at least, to the old ideals of the French Revolution, 'liberty, equality, fraternity', but they freely confess that the realization of these ideals in the social life of Western countries still remains very incomplete."* [1] Later, he backflips on his assertion that *'their world is purely human and secular'* (and this is where I tend to agree with him): *"The modern West, I am arguing, is the legacy of Christianity, and in particular of two central doctrines: the creation and preservation of the world by God, and the final definitive incarnation of God in the man Jesus Christ."* [2] Well, I say I *tend* to agree with him and it is because of the words 'final definitive *incarnation* of God' in Jesus. The modern West does not agree with the incarnation of God in Jesus. The modern West may believe in a God to some extent (maybe not God the Father), and believes in the teachings of Jesus Christ without necessarily believing he was God. In fact, I am pretty sure the West has generally discarded that notion, together with the rest of the dogma of the Church. On the other hand, I believe saying that God has incarnated definitively and finally in humanity is very presumptuous, if that is what he wants to say.

Individually, the West is a state of mind. Authors like Miller and Kerouac and Hemingway, for instance, are thoroughly Western authors. By the same token, nobody could deny that Nabokov, a Russian who lived in Western Europe, or Cortázar, Latin American to the core, are also Western authors. In terms of countries and regions, pretty much like the Roman Empire from which it evolved, the West is far from a homogeneous bloc. There are gradations. But when we talk of Western countries, 'Western' is synonymous with 'advanced'. And I would venture it is also possible to say that the countries that led the way in terms of scientific and technological advance that were mostly Protestant or a mix of Protestant and Catholic. Culturally, Australia, Canada and the United States are definitely part of the European West. They are countries that have historically remained liberal democracies. What distinguishes them from other countries is their Western European culture and traditions, which of course include Christianity as one of its main historical elements.

If we are to believe in surveys and statistics, the West is slowly abandoning its organised religion. This worries people. In a recent article about Christianity in England in The London Times, Daniel Finkelstein gave a some idea of how that may constitute a problem: *"The decline of religion is not only a liberation. There is a troubling aspect to it too."* [3] Finkelstein summarises his concern in very few words: *"I am not arguing that charity, community and fellow feeling are impossible without religion; only that we are living through a time of great change and should appreciate that we are."* [4] What Finkelstein says applies to the West in general. According to this view, it is a Western crisis (and by this he probably means a time of uncertainty between two stable periods, a time when a decision has to be made, a crossroads). This may not be as bleak as Finkelstein points out, but there is a loss, and a general feeling of disenchantment. Tom Holland says: *"The West, increasingly empty though the pews may be, remains firmly moored to its Christian past."* [5] That may be clearly noticed during Christmas, Epiphany, Easter, etc. Many complain that those holidays have become something commercial and, it is true, there is a great commercial influence in them. However, the spirit is there. The Western individual, the Western family, continues to maintain a strong connection with the teachings of Jesus Christ.

Don Cupitt explains: *"As Christianity fulfils its historical task by imprinting all this material upon us, it secularizes itself into Western culture which already increasingly belongs not just to Europe and 'the English-speaking world', but to all human beings everywhere. As this process continues, the old ecclesiastical type of Christianity becomes redundant and disappears, but culturally objectified Christianity goes on and will go on unstoppably until its task is done. Already it is much more fully and generously catholic than 'Catholicism' could ever have hoped to become."* [6]

CHRISTIANITY, THE INDIVIDUAL
AND THE WEST

*A*s I begin to write this, I imagine a man sitting at his desk, carefully cutting up a Bible and pasting selected passages onto a copybook; the moment is not too difficult to visualise: it's early 19th century, 1803 to be precise and the tall, fine-featured man is taking some time off of his extremely busy schedule to attend to his spiritual life. Although at that point, in his own words, he was *'overwhelmed with other business'*, Thomas Jefferson, third President of the United States, had decided to enjoy a break from his official duties in order to produce his own version of the Gospels.

Jefferson, a rare kind of polymath, inventor, author, designer, architect, farmer, diplomat, politician, statesman, had put his unusual genius at work in the design of Gospels that would reflect his own beliefs. He was interested in Jesus' teachings, but rejected all the supernatural elements of the New Testament which he considered irrational, so he removed any passages that included miracles, apparitions of angels, the virgin birth, the ascension of Christ, mentions of Jesus as God, the Trinity, etc., from the book. He called it *The philosophy of Jesus of Nazareth, extracted from the account of his life and doctrines, as given by Matthew, Mark, Luke and John; being an abridgment of the New Testament for the use of the Indians, unembarrassed with matters of fact or faith beyond the level of their comprehension.* In spite of the grandiose title, he ended up keeping the book for his own private use. Seventeen years later he wrote an edited version, which included Latin, Greek and French versions of the text. It is called *The life and morals of Jesus of Nazareth*, and is now known as *The Jefferson Bible*.

Jefferson was a supremely rational man, a man of the Enlightenment. His ideas summarise what is currently Christian belief in the West: arguably, most people in the modern West tend to follow the moral teachings of Jesus but reject the paranormal events that the Gospels allege occurred during his lifetime.

It is difficult to mention Jefferson without having to acknowledge his other, darker, side: he was a rich slave owner who had a long relationship with one of his slaves, beautiful Sally Hemings, with whom he fathered six children. The children were assigned household chores in Monticello, Jefferson's residence, and remained slaves and footmen until Jefferson's death in 1823. Many judge him as the person who wrote the Declaration of Independence and overtly proclaimed his rectitude and morals, Christian or otherwise, while profiting from slavery and leading a double life with a slave/concubine. His feeling of guilt and his contrition about Sally and the children, and his unease in that respect, are much easier to understand if we try to put ourselves in the shoes of a person of the 18th and early 19th centuries, with all the moral limitations that perspective implies. Slavery, racism and sexism were generally accepted, and having a concubine was no big deal.

In any case, Jefferson remains an undisputed genius, one of the Fathers of the Independence of the United States, a man who could not accept the religious deceptions of previous times and had the selective mind, strength of character, and the vision to publish something like *The life and morals of Jesus of Nazareth*.

Two centuries later, in his book *The meaning of the West*, Don Cupitt reiterates Jefferson's ideas and suggests that they now represent Christianity; the fact that Jesus' teachings, and very little else, constitute the main basis of our Western morals: *"... I have been suggesting that in the modern West the post-metaphysical, non-theistic and radical Christian vision of the Kingdom of God has triumphed."*[1]

Many in the West appear to be happy to see doctrinal Christianity disappear in the background. Given all the disappointments the Church has given us, it is understandable. But in terms of religious culture it is also simplistic. We repeat, it would be impossible to renounce Christianity altogether, as many atheists naïvely propose, without destroying Western civilisation. Christianity is an integral part not just of our mores and ethics, of our art, but also of our way of thinking and living. And this goes beyond our history, calendar, our holidays, and our languages. Yes, religion has influenced and continues to influence our civilisation in good and bad ways. It is inbuilt in every cell of our being: it cannot be eradicated without killing the host. Thinking about Christianity as an external issue is, partially and paradoxically, a result of Christianity.

This self-identification of Christians as Christians at the DNA level is what Don Cupitt calls *'the indelible'*. *"In summary, I stick with the view that the postmodern West is secularized Christianity.*

Since the Enlightenment, a vast number of people have supposed that one can reject Christian dogma and leave the Church – and thereafter have no further connection with Christianity. Not so. We remain what Christianity has made us, and in many respects the postmodern West is more Christian than ever. If you are a Westerner and you are committed to Western values, then you are a Christian. A 'crusader-zionist', indeed, says Mr Bin Laden indignantly, and he's right again." [2]

I totally subscribe to Cupitt's idea. We live in a historical continuum that commences with the Bible and reaches our current era.

Organised religion became gradually obsolete with the development of critical thinking. The Enlightenment as we know defied much of the irrationality of Christian dogma. As we have seen, Thomas Jefferson famously came up with the *Jefferson Bible*, from which he excised all miracles and angelic revelations. Darwin probably hammered the last nail in that coffin. Christian values, however, continue in the West in a secular but pervasive form.

In his book *The Lexus and the olive tree* advocating globalisation in 1999, Thomas L Friedman expressed an extraordinary view coming from an economist: he said that the origin of the quests for material betterment and for individual and communal identity went all the way back to Genesis. Those quests, he wrote, play an important role in the international system of globalisation. Arguably, Western countries offer a better lifestyle than other countries. What is undeniable now is that many individuals (and sometimes multitudes) cross borders looking for that better life, and those movements create tensions. Many refugees want the financial benefits of the West without sacrificing any part of their culture. The problem is that living in the West requires an acceptance of the freedoms of others, which is incompatible with Islam, for instance, the original culture of the majority of refugees.

Where do we go from here? What led us to this point? All those questions require answers ... and strangely enough some of the answers may be found in the Book of Genesis. There are all sorts of hidden questions in the history of our civilisation, the most important civilisation the world has ever seen. Many of them have to do with Christianity. Whether we believe in God or not is totally irrelevant. What is important is the way belief has influenced our thought as a community.

As we have seen, this book touches on religion but is not quite about religion. It is not theology. Among other things, it is about how Christianity has shaped Western culture (or actually *is* Western culture). And it is about tracing some connections between the different searches for the meaning of the soul, or of consciousness, and the meaning of God. It has been a story full of mistakes, wrong choices, mess-ups, politicking and deceit.

Disparaging religion has been a fashionable sport for some decades, and the subject has attracted quite a few bestselling authors. Certainly, people like Dawkins and Hitchens have devoted their lives to the cause: religion has long been the enemy of progress, the enemy of science. In the age of Internet, religion appears to be an anachronism, but what many scientists and atheists do not seem to realise is that Christianity is part and parcel of their paradigm. They are poles on opposite sides of the same philosophical perspective, that's all.

The ancient Greeks, the originators of Western thought, were great individualists. Through the ballot, they were the first to give individuals the power of electing the people who would govern them, the main basis of liberal democracy. The connection between Greek thought and Christianity is not a tenuous one. In fact, it is very strong. The Bible reached the West through Greek translations. The reason for that is that the Jews of the Hellenistic Diaspora (which is a Greek word) were fluent Greek speakers. Many of them had forgotten Aramaic and Hebrew, the languages of their parents. Those Jews, and many more Gentiles of course, were among the first to convert to Christianity. But there is more, there is a much stronger connection: St Paul, the real creator of the religion, as we have seen, was born in the Hellenistic province of Cilicia, spoke Greek and spent his formative years there. He obviously was very familiar with the concept of soul (*psyche*) as envisaged by Greek thinkers. The term is used often in the New Testament. The idea was relatively alien to the Hebrews. The Jewish Bible makes reference to the human soul on occasion, but the meaning is totally different. Their idea of soul is more related to life, the life that God breathes into Adam, for instance, and the Hebrew word (*nephesh*) has totally different connotations. When St Paul returned to Palestine, he interpreted the Jewish Bible in a very Greek fashion. To summarise, Christianity is the result of a marriage between Hebrew tradition and Greek thought.

It is time many people in the West come to the realisation that Christianity had to be there for science and technology, and Western culture in general, to develop the way they have. This is no vindication or eulogy of doctrinal Christianity. As it often happens in history, there was no project, no volition involved. Christianity just happened to be there at the time. And its philosophical foundations happened to be conducive to observation of the kind required by science. And, surprise,

surprise... the concept of the 'individual' was at the centre of the religion that brought us the West.

In Western thought, science and philosophy run almost parallel courses as they are both based on the observation of nature. The observer has to be external to the object being observed. This is a principle of Aristotelian philosophy. According to it, reality is observable and it is objective.

That great construct of the Western mind, objective reality, resulted in a culture where individuals were witnesses of the universe that surrounded them. Their skin was the boundary between them and that strange 'otherness' that was there to be analysed and understood.

Greek philosophers were originally the great observers of reality, but the concept of individual consciousness that was about to take hold in the Roman world would come from Christianity.

Before the Romans had become the virtual owners of the Mediterranean and Christianity the religion of the Empire, Greek was the language used not only by philosophers, but also by the Roman elites. Julius Caesar spoke Greek and Marcus Aurelius wrote his *Meditations* in Greek. By the Early Middle Ages, however, Greek texts had almost disappeared and only partial Latin translations of Greek philosophy were available. The original works of the Greek philosophers could only be found in Byzantium.

There are different versions as to what happened next, one is that the Arabs of the Abbasid Caliphate, in Baghdad, became interested in Greek philosophy for their own purposes and commissioned Christian translators to turn the Greek classics into Arabic. Aristotle, according to this version, returned to

Western Europe in a roundabout way: interest in Latin translations of Averroes an Andalusian Muslim who wrote commentaries of Aristotle's works quickly resulted in a renewed interest in everything Greek. Another version is that Greek thought was re-discovered through Venice, when the Byzantine intelligentsia fled the Turkish invasion. That was the beginning of what was called the 'Renaissance', the rebirth. In any case, in Middle-Age Europe, after Aristotle was discovered again, one of the main proponents of Aristotelian thought was Thomas Aquinas, who also happened to be the main Christian philosopher of all times. Their combined teachings are known as Aristotelian-Thomistic. Modern science developed on the basis of Aristotelian-Thomistic thought.

Modern science requires the predictability and stability of the physical world that became apparent from questions posed by these two philosophers. The nominalist ideas of William of Ockham, another medieval friar, gave science its most important philosophical basis.

In that respect, Don Cupitt tells us: *"God promises that the natural world will be regular and law-abiding, and then gives to humans through a great prophet the system of sacred Law that they are to live by. Thus God gives to humans an orderly cosmology, and therewith some participation in his own knowledge and understanding of the created order."* [3]

Science needs nature to be ordered according to laws. It needs somebody observing nature from the outside. Indeed, objective reality. Newton's gravitational theory is based on objective reality. Darwin's theory of the evolution of the species is based on objective reality. All science is based on it.

At the beginning, the individual found him or herself immersed in this incredible universe that was totally incomprehensible. Inquisitiveness, curiosity, and methodical study did the rest.

The first monotheistic religion, Judaism, offered some answers as to who the creator of the universe was, how to behave in society, what was expected of the individual, but offered no hope at the time of death. You had to be contented with your life in this world. There was nothing after that. Christianity adopted the basis of Judaism but it also offered an individual soul that would never die. That was a game changer.

Egyptians believed in life after death in a physical sense, hence mummification. Christianity introduced a new kind of hope through the notion of the individual immortal soul. There was an afterlife and the individual was going to be there to enjoy it forever. Before Christianity, the individual had never received so much attention. In doing so, Christianity fostered individuality, a uniquely Western feature. One might even go as far as suggesting that Christianity 'invented' the notion of the individual, pretty much like the troubadours of Provence 'invented' the notion of romantic love. Some will think that this is an exaggeration, but it is as close to the mark as it comes. I will return to this point, as romantic love (and the exaltation of women as superior beings) is also a uniquely Western and Christian phenomenon.

CHRISTIANITY AND THE CREATION OF THE INDIVIDUAL SOUL

As we all know, science, that by-product of superstition, evolved through critical thinking (together with philosophy, the other discipline of Western thought). Yes, science and philosophy grew out of the Renaissance and the Enlightenment, were heavily influenced by Christianity, and were the origin of the economic formula for Western growth and development.

Originally, there was some contribution to science from the East but, in general, the largest development of science and technology occurred in the Christian West. We can say with some degree of certainty that such a development led to technology, the industrial revolution and capitalism as we know it. Max Weber explained it in detail in *The Protestant ethic and the spirit of capitalism*. However, Weber erroneously believed that Western culture began placing its emphasis on the individual only after Martin Luther's Reformation in the sixteenth century. Although there is some truth to that assertion, the Reformation did not appear spontaneously; it was not an isolated phenomenon; as we have discussed, the emphasis on the individual began with St Paul's promise of eternal individual salvation in Jesus Christ. No one before then had even considered the relationship between the individual and God. A Christian slave, a woman, a prostitute, could eventually share heaven with God. This was a unique Pauline idea, one that he applied when he misinterpreted or misrepresented the myth of the Garden of Eden and retrofitted into it his incredible Judaeo-Christian redemption twist.

When analysing the rise of individualism in Western Europe, those who place all the emphasis on Martin Luther tend to ignore major phenomena that preceded him without which his ecclesiastic revolution would have been impossible. The Renaissance, which was centred in Florence and flourished many decades before him, had an undoubted humanistic emphasis on individual beauty and independence, and created a magnificent banking system and a bourgeois-centred mercantile infrastructure that resulted in the growth of the market economy in Medieval Europe. The invention of mechanical-movable-type printing by Johannes Gutenberg in 1439, that is, almost a century before Luther, was indeed essential for the spread of his Reformation, not a result of it.

In any case, if we analyse the evolution of Western thought, there is no escaping from the fact that Christian belief played an important part in it.

Nowadays, except for a few fundamentalists, everyone accepts evolution as a fact. Thanks to Darwin and all the scientists that followed him, we know we are evolved apes.

Aristotle defined humans as *'zoon politikon' ('social animals')*. Quite clearly, during his lifetime, the idea of separateness between humans and animals had not been introduced yet. It is clear that until then the Greeks had thought consciousness (*psyche*) was something we had acquired somehow but did not make us different from other mammals, for instance. We are in the 21st century and, regardless of the advances of knowledge, that Christian feeling of separateness remains strong among certain believers. It is very difficult, in spite of Hitchens' efforts (he used to refer to humans as 'mammals'), to think of ourselves as animals. How did that happen? Why is this notion of separateness so persistent? When did we decide that? Those are some of the questions we are analysing.

Let's see: human beings became physically separate from wild animals when they started living in cities. Even though some urban dwellers hunted, their everyday lives took place within urban confines.

Urbanisation began from 8,000 to 10,000 years ago, with cities like Mohenjo-Daro and Jericho; the main parts of the Jewish Bible were arguably written some 700 years BC, give or take some centuries, (the New Testament was probably written and compiled no later than 120 AD). As we have said before, if one interprets the *Tanakh* using critical thinking, it states quite clearly and repeatedly that we are evolved animals and nothing but animals, so the beginning of urbanisation was not the moment when separation human/animal supposedly happened.

The fact that a human being was deified meant indeed that we were very special, but the deification of Jesus Christ at the First Council of Nicaea was not the moment when that notion of separation appeared either. Deifications and apotheoses had occurred before, in Greece and Rome, and those of many pharaohs. Nicaea was a consequence rather than a cause, if you like. It was the result of more than three hundred years of incubation.

The conversion of St Paul to Jesus of Nazareth's tiny, charismatic, sect of Judaism, was probably the beginning of the process. More precisely, the trigger appears to have been Paul's seminal but quirky interpretation of the Book of Genesis. That interpretation was meant to add extra 'spirituality' to a religion whose time and scope had passed. Old Judaism, the religion of the Sadducees, of the Roman province of Judea, the religion of the Temple, with its tribal, self-imposed limits, needed a massive change to metamorphose into the new all-embracing faith that would become the official religion of the Roman Empire.

Paul was the first to discuss the human soul as a phenomenon that was separate from the rest of the animals. Christianity introduced it. So, we can say that the ancient Hebrews believed in a probably less drastic version of evolution of the species. But I have discussed that in detail.

Maybe we can also say that, until Darwin, nobody challenged the Christian interpretation of the Book of Genesis with its many unanswered riddles and its philosophical influence on the West. Darwin's challenge to Christian creation came in a way totally unrelated to religion, through scientific reasoning and as a consequence of his inquisitiveness. Surprisingly, only Isaac Asimov attempted a thorough, rational analysis of the Book of Genesis, if not quite an exegesis. The book was *In the beginning*. That was in 1981. There was also La Peyrère, centuries before him, but his conclusions were not quite as logical.

Through his strange interpretation of Genesis, St Paul introduced the spiritual change needed for the development of science, technology and, eventually, capitalism in the West. In other words, science, much to atheists' chagrin, is immanently bound to Christianity.

According to the Pauline interpretation of Genesis, species were effectively declared immutable. Human beings had been originally immortal (!) and became mortal as a way of punishment for their original sin. It was decided, that they had been created separately and possessed an individual soul that was immortal, one of the ramifications of which was the exaltation of the human individual with his or her personal consciousness. Individuality is, indeed, one of the bases of Western civilisation. It would be logical to venture that the Christian interpretation of the *Torah* long before the Reformation was the historical event that gave way to Western culture.

Centuries later, following in St Paul's footsteps, people like Polycarp, Clement, Irenaeus, Alexander and Augustine – the Fathers of the Church – made decisions regarding Christianity and what became its dogma: they chose what would be included in the Christian Bible and how the *Torah* would be interpreted.

Throughout its early history, the Church persecuted all other versions of Christianity: they were what the Church called 'heresies'. Those times were later known as the Dark Ages. Astrology and alchemy appeared, almost unnoticed, on the scene. They developed into astronomy and chemistry and influenced other disciplines. Science crept in slowly, out of a nebula of superstition.

The Western way of life evolved strangely. There was this dance, where religion, philosophy, art, and eventually science, acting pretty much like the four bases of Western DNA, intertwined to form the double helix of our culture.

If one reads the *Tanakh* carefully, it becomes apparent that the Hebrews (as was most probably the case with other ancient peoples) knew, took for granted, or maybe suspected, that they were just like other animals, that they were primates. Or at least they did not know they were anything but. They were apes that wore clothes, made tools and could speak. There was no other reality. Why would humans be separate when there were so many traits shared with the rest of the animals, when there were so many clues that they were not? The separation was indeed extremely counter-intuitive. We can even claim that the original monotheistic religion, the religion of the Sadducees and the Temple, the one that provided the basis for modern Judaism, Christianity and Islam, coincided with Darwin to some extent (I have elaborated on this point). Then

St Paul introduced Plato's notion of the individual immortal soul. Human beings became officially separate from the rest of nature this was a unique error, or deception perhaps, that helped foster spirituality in the West. A butterfly had flapped its wings and that would eventually create a huge storm.

The afterlife had been imagined by other cultures in a more pedestrian fashion. The Egyptians, as we have said, were obsessed with death and what comes after it. In their case the notion was not as imaginative. It was basically more materialistic than Christianity. The idea of an eternal afterlife was the trigger for the growth of the tiny Jewish sect that eventually morphed into a world religion. The idea of the individual soul was definitely what created the West as we know it today, which obviously included the Industrial Revolution and Capitalism.

GOD AS A POSSIBILITY

In the West we are presented with two alternatives that involve an external, analytical view of the universe: a) The religious one is that there is a God that has given us a soul and has put us in charge of the universe; b) the scientific one, or the other pole of the paradigm, is that there is no god but that the universe is still an external object of study that we must conquer.

Robert Wright gives us a hint that there may be a third alternative, this time one that, without being anthropocentric, appears to include humans as an integral, active, part of the universe: *"On the one hand, I think gods arose as an illusion, and the subsequent history of the idea of god is, in some sense, the evolution of an illusion. On the other hand: (1) the story of this evolution itself points to the existence of something you can meaningfully call divinity; and (2) the 'illusion', in the course of evolving, has gotten streamlined in a way that moved it closer to plausibility. In both these senses, the illusion has gotten less and less illusory."* [1]

If I understand this correctly, what Wright appears to be saying here is that although we have been looking at it from a twisted perspective, the fact that we have created a hologram of god may in itself be God.

Some years ago, Stephen Hawking pontificated that God was unnecessary.

Hawking's comment appears to be directed at the anthropocentrism of doctrinal Christianity. The question should not be whether we need a God. The assumption should be that God might still be there even if we do not need a God. The existence of a deity like the God of the Enlightenment would at least provide a purpose, which Higgs boson could never do with its random explanation for the creation of the universe. What was unnecessary, I would say to Professor Hawking, was the deception that came with the doctrine that the Church added to Jesus' message.

The crux of the matter is that once all the deception of organised Christianity was uncovered, once we knew things were not quite what we were told they were (the angel with a toupee) it was impossible to go back to that primeval innocence of Adam and Eve, if you like. The aspect of Christianity that cannot be denied is that it is immanent to the West and that the West cannot reject it altogether, even if it wanted to. That aspect is what has provided the ethical and moral basis for our culture. Science has not disproved a number of things posited by Christianity. An unknown actor beyond our comprehension could have created the universe. The universe may have a purpose. Consciousness is as much of a mystery to religion as it is to science. We keep on discovering: Wright propounds: *"... but always some notion of the divine has survived the encounter with science. The notion has had to change, but that's no indictment of religion. After all, science has changed relentlessly, revising if not discarding old theories, and none of us think of that as an indictment of science. On the contrary, we think this ongoing adaptation is carrying science closer to the truth."* [2]

A collective consciousness, such as Spinoza and many others proposed, is quite compatible with the concept of the Holy Spirit. And no doubt the teachings of Jesus, the man, have given us guidance for over two millennia of Western civilisation. Maybe this is the time for winnowing. Maybe it is time to discern and separate wheat from chaff. Quite evidently, the teachings of Jesus Christ are more than just salvageable. The way I see it, they are the operating system of Western culture.

AFTERWORD

We have seen how the modern world, with its science and its technology mostly imagined and constructed in the West is the direct result of Christianity.

Something even more paradoxical: the secularisation of the world seems to have also grown out of Christian teachings.

In the Introduction I say, among other things, that modern individualism, capitalism, democratic and international institutions, globalisation, free trade, civil rights and atheism in summary, all that represents the West, are the direct result of Christianity. Without Christianity none of those institutions would have existed. Rather than a paradox, this would seem to include something implausible or improbable. A Christian atheism? ... an oxymoron, a contradiction in terms. Maybe some followers of scientism would want to deny that. My idea, however beginning with the Pauline interpretation of the myth of Adam and Eve is so implausible or improbable as the fact that a human being could have grown out of an amoeba. It's all a matter of evolution. And interpretation.

Christianity broke away from all religious canons of its times. Primitive religions were exclusive, that is, national or tribal. The also reflected the dynamics of the times. Justice was retributive. Anyone who did anything against society had to pay for it mimetically. Talion Law would apply, i.e., there was retaliation: *"an eye for an eye and a tooth for a tooth"*.

In religious terms, communal violence was directed towards a sole innocent victim. There was a *"sacrifice"*, that is, that kind of singularised vengeance was sacralised in a rite through which the fault or sin that had been committed would be atoned. Christ taught that one should turn the other cheek, and Paul, in turn, converted the Son of the sole God of Judaism, into God himself, but also into a victim.

Paul demonstrated something that should have been evident but wasn't in archaic religions: sacrifice meant a violent injustice. Until that moment religions had looked for scapegoats without quite understanding why they were doing it. Christianity, turning against the Temple, against the Sadducees, showed that the victim was innocent (as Jesus Christ was) and that the existing religious order needed a radical change. Violence against the victim was unnecessary. The non-violent radicalisation of religion was reflected in a new vision of the social order. That phenomenon, exclusively Christian, was the beginning of the world we know nowadays.

At the beginning of the book I propose that the argument has always been based on the fact that relativism, acceptance, inclusivity, and logic are all attributes of atheism, while it is generally accepted that religion is conservative, hegemonic and totalitarian; that religious faith is obscurantist by definition. It is true that rationalism and Christianity haven't always known how to live and grow together.

The general belief is that Christianity and science are antithetical concepts, elements of different paradigms. What I have proposed in this book is that they are elements of the same paradigm, which we could call "Western and Christian", and that science, as it has developed in the West, could not have existed without a Christian basis.

The idea still exists that the Church, an all-powerful organisation, obstructed science and did the impossible to stop its advance. What is not remembered nowadays is that the Church founded many European universities and during the Middle Ages most scientists were monks, especially because most books were the property of monasteries, in whose libraries they were kept and copied. During the Middle Ages there was a metaphor: that it was possible to reach the mind of God in two ways, one was through the Scriptures, and the other one was studying the book of Nature.

It is obvious that the Church has kept some common parts it had with archaic religions and that it has not done all it could have done towards the advancement of humanity. Until the Enlightenment, unfortunately, conditions were not very favourable: According to Girard: *"... the Enlightenment was a turning point, when the Christian and Western portions of humanity realized that the world was changing, that people were more free, that there was greater scope for action on the part of mankind... But the erroneous belief took hold that this was only the upshot of the actions of men, of individual geniuses or the genius of the human species in general."* [1]

I do not totally agree with Girard. I believe the Church is only the official face of Christianity, the organised religion that needs directives and prohibitions. The idea has some value. The most visible extremes of that type of reality are orthodox

Judaism and Islam, much more prescriptive than Christianity or rabbinical Judaism. Of course we need morals and ethics. The way I see it, however, human beings are nurtured by love and charity and resent restrictions, especially when they are arbitrary and are opposed to the enjoyment of life.

True Christianity does not claim to excuse human nature but to redeem it. No doubt, Christianity demands faith in the human being.

Of course, in order to share our existence in society, to be well behaved, we need guidelines and, up to a point, some prescription but, above all, precepts.

I believe the norms provided by non-religious legislation, with all their Christian basis, appear to be enough for Western society to function.

If we read Girard: *"In this connection, it is becoming clearer all the time that religion defeats philosophy and outstrips it. In fact, the various philosophies are practically dead on their feet; the ideologies are virtually defunct; political theories are almost at an end; and faith in science as a substitute for religion is by now a hollow faith indeed. There is a new felt need for religion."* [2]

I do not share totally, but I believe there is some truth in what he says. In reality, I feel that what I want to say is closer to Vattimo: *"... there is a return to religion today because people have realized that all the forms of knowledge regarded as definitive have turned out to be dependent on historical paradigms, on various kinds of reckoning social, political, ideological and so on. No longer can we assert that since science knows nothing of God, God does not exist."* [3]

What I see is not a return to organised religion as such, but a larger acceptance of the possibility of the deity. That is, that an intellectual or a scientist may affirm his or her belief in deism such as Voltaire's without being totally shunned by their peers. That larger acceptance of a Jeffersonian Christianity, of a Bible without miracles or supernatural phenomena totally unacceptable to sophisticated knowledge nowadays is, I believe, proof that Western Christianity has evolved towards its cultural phase.

That third stage of Christianity that Joachim da Fiore suspected/prophesied, the Age of the Holy Spirit, whose rational embryo was already present in Saul of Tarsus, is the reality we live nowadays. A Christianity of precepts rather than prescriptions, a Christianity not diluted but rather foreseen, logical and anti-dogma.

It would seem, then, that the West now prepared to share everything with the rest of the world is based on a logical and inclusive historical foundation, and that Christianity more than survives in its institutions.

THE HOLY SPIRIT

ACKNOWLEDGMENTS

As happens to those of us who write something, there is always somebody we have to thank for having advised us, for their work, for their time. In the case of *The Myth of Adam and Eve*, I have to thank Inés firstly, as I write when I dedicate it to her, because she put up with my crazy ideas, because she read the original in English and the version in Spanish and helped with the proofing. Because she gave me many tips that were extremely useful, and because she had to hear on countless occasions my soliloquies and all the times I read aloud.

I also want to thank Anni Boerr, friend and schoolmate from high school, who not only had kindness and was good enough to read the Spanish manuscript, but also recommended other possible readers and critics. I am eternally grateful to her.

The readers, also friends and schoolmates, had the patience to read and make suggestions, which were invaluable. Many thanks, Pethie Hall, Tina Echazarreta and Chichita Giraldez.

My siblings, Patocho and Queque Pintos-López read parts of this version and the translation. Zoe McKenzie, Robyn Dwyer and Rod Haedo also read parts of the English version. To all of them, my thanks.

INDEX

A

Abraham, 8, 52, 58, 67, 77

Aeneas, 21

Ahaz, 15

Alexander of Alexandria, 85, 93, 94, 98, 150

Asimov, Isaac, 26, 35, 36, 38, 39, 47, 150

Aslan, Reza, 40, 62, 66, 68, 73, 78, 79, 94, 114, 124

Athanasius of Alexandria, 85, 94, 95

Averroes, 145

B

Bishop Eusebius of Nicomedia, 93

Bishop Hosius of Cordova, 92, 93, 95

Buck, Peter, 134

C

Cain, 35, 36, 39, 41

Calvin, John, 86, 113, 126

Caravaggio, 134

Charles VIII of France, 98

Comte de Buffon, 116

Constantine, 5, 80, 92, 93, 94, 96

Cupitt, Don, 102, 108, 136, 138, 140, 141, 145

D

da Fiore, Joachim, 97, 158

David, 13, 14, 15, 67

Dawkins, Richard, 48, 49, 87, 106, 109, 110, 111, 112, 113, 115, 122, 143

de Botton, Alain, 107, 115, 127, 130

de Medici, Lorenzo, 98

della Mirandola, Pico, 98

Denisovans, 38, 39, 53

Descartes, René, 31

Desmond, Adrian, 119

Dhandwar, Tarsem Singh, 134

Diocletian, 80, 92

E

Ecclesiastes, 23, 24, 122, 163

Elector Frederick the Wise, 99

Exodus, 17

F

Fromm, Eric, 105

G

García Márquez, Gabriel, 134

George Steiner, 3

Girard, René, 157, 158

Grayling, A C, 108, 109, 114

Greenblatt, Stephen, 20, 35, 43, 46, 49, 117, 124

H

Hammurabi, 17

Hemingway, Ernest, 137

Hezekiah, 15, 16, 17, 18, 51, 82

Higgs Boson, 107, 132

Hitchens, Christopher, 46, 48, 123, 124, 128, 129, 130, 132, 143, 148

Hobbes, Thomas, 33, 107

Holland, Tom, 113, 120, 138

Homer, 21

Homo Erectus, 27

Homo Sapiens, 27, 28, 32, 34

Huxley, Thomas, 123

I

Irenaeus of Lyons, 84

J

Jackson, Stonewall, 128

James, Craig A, 111

Jefferson, Thomas, 139, 140, 141

Jeroboam, 14

Jesus, 9, 10, 40, 42, 51, 54, 55, 56, 58, 59, 60, 61, 62, 64, 65, 66, 67, 68, 69, 70, 71, 72, 73, 74, 75, 76, 77, 78, 80, 81, 83, 84, 85, 87, 89, 90, 91, 93, 94, 95, 96, 97, 100, 109, 111, 116, 119, 126, 129, 131, 136, 138, 139, 140, 147, 149, 154, 156

Julius Caesar, 144

K

Keane, Bernard, 100

Kerouac, Jack, 137

Kierkegaard, Søren, 107

L

La Peyrère, Isaac, 35, 36, 150

Lee, Robert E, 128

Leviticus, 16, 17

Licinius, 92

Lorenzo the Magnificent. *See* de Medici, Lorenzo

Lucretius, 50, 116, 117, 163

Luther, Martin, 86

M

Marduk, 17

Margaret of Navarre, 97

Martin Luther, 5, 55, 97, 99, 100, 113, 147

Max Weber, 7, 19, 147

Metaxas, Eric, 100

Miller, Arthur, 137

Moore, James, 119

Moses, 8, 12, 13, 24, 78, 87, 89, 131

N

Neanderthals, 38, 39, 52

Newton, Sir Isaac, 146

Nicholas of Myra, 95, *See* Nicholas of Myra, *See* St Nicholas, *See* Santa Claus

O

Ockham, William of, 145

Origen Adamantios, 85

P

Pagels, Elaine, 84, 86

Paine, Thomas, 106

Paul, Diane B, 119

Pentateuch, 13, 18, 65

Pope Alexander VI, 98, 99

Pope Leo X, 100

Pope Pius XII, 126

R

Rehoboam, 14

Rubenstein, Richard, 80, 89, 93, 94, 95

Russell, Bertrand, 107

S

Sagan, Carl, 26

Samson, 16

Savonarola, Girolamo, 98, 99

Solomon, 13, 14, 15

Spinoza, Baruch, 154

St Augustine, 29, 31, 49, 86, 113, 150

St Clement, 150

St John the Baptist, 5, 51, 60, 61, 69, 73, 87

St Paul, 7, 9, 11, 19, 20, 29, 31, 39, 42, 44, 45, 47, 48, 49, 53, 54, 55, 56, 57, 58, 60, 64, 73, 75, 76, 77, 78, 79, 80, 83, 94, 101, 111, 115, 117, 143, 147, 149, 150, 151

St Polycarp, 150

St Thomas Aquinas, 56, 145

Stipe, 134, 135

T

Tanach, 9, 11, 13, 40, 46, 58, 115

Theodosius, 80, 92

Torah, 9, 12, 13, 17, 18, 19, 26, 28, 31, 33, 39, 40, 41, 44, 45, 47, 49, 51, 52, 58, 60, 62, 64, 78, 80, 81, 83, 86, 94, 96, 117, 132, 133, 150

V

Vattimo, Gianni, 104, 158

Vermes, Geza, 73, 76, 83, 84, 87, 88, 96

Virgil, 21

Voltaire, 106, 158

W

Wedgewood, Emma, 117

Wittgenstein, Ludwig, 104, 107

Wright, Robert, 25, 38, 108, 109, 112, 122, 125, 126, 131, 133, 153, 154

Y

Yahweh, 25, 29, 33, 58, 73, 81, 87, 90, 106, 109, 111, 131, 132

Z

Zwingli, Ulrich, 113

NOTES

3. MYTH

1. GREENBLATT, Stephen – *The rise and fall of Adam and Eve*, p.17 – W.W. Norton & Company (2017)

5. THE MYTH OF ADAM & EVE

1. (Ecclesiastes III:18-20) King James Version
2. (Ecclesiastes III:21-22) King James Version
3. ASIMOV, Isaac – *In the beginning*, p.289, eBook
4. Genesis (III:19) King James Version
5. Genesis (III:17) King James Version

6. AWARENESS OF MORTALITY

1. HOBBES, Thomas – *Leviathan*, pp. 325-326 – Collier Macmillan Publishers (1977)

7. THE MYSTERY OF CAIN'S WIFE

1. GREENBLATT, Stephen – *The rise and fall of Adam and Eve*, p.232 – W.W. Norton & Company (2017)
2. ASIMOV, Isaac – *In the beginning*, p.320, eBook

8. HOW HUMANITY SPREAD AMONG THE HOMININS

1. (Genesis VI: 1-4) King James Version
2. ASIMOV, Isaac – *In the beginning*, pp.359-360, eBook
3. WRIGHT, Robert – *The evolution of god* , p.11 – Back Bay Books (2009)
4. ASIMOV, Isaac – *In the beginning*, p.361, eBook
5. ASLAN, Reza – *Zealot* , p.136 – Random House (2013)

9. CHRISTIAN INTERPRETATION OF THE BOOK OF GENESIS

1. GREENBLATT, Stephen – *The rise and fall of Adam and Eve*, p.8 – W.W. Norton & Company (2017)
    PLATO – The republic, p. 320 – Everyman (1995)
    GREENBLATT, Stephen – *The rise and fall of Adam and Eve*, p.8 – W.W. Norton & Company (2017)
2. BLOOM, Harold – *Take arms against a sea of troubles*, p.95 – Yale University Press, 2020
3. GREENBLATT, Stephen – *The rise and fall of Adam and Eve*, p.39 – W.W. Norton & Company (2017)
4. ASIMOV, Isaac – *In the beginning*, pp.212-213, eBook
5. DAWKINS, Richard – *The god delusion*, p. 251 – Bantam Press (2006)
6. DAWKINS, Richard – *The god delusion*, p. 251 – Bantam Press (2006)
7. GREENBLATT, Stephen – *The rise and fall of Adam and Eve*, p.126 – W.W. Norton & Company (2017)

10. HUMANS AS PRIMATES

1. LUCRETIUS (Titus Lucretius Carus) – *De rerum natura*, p. 398 - eBook
2. MOSER, Stephanie – *Ancestral Images: The Iconography of Human Origins* – p.43 – Cornell University Press (1998)
3. MOSER, Stephanie – *Ancestral Images: The Iconography of Human Origins* – pp.169-170– Cornell University Press (1998)
4. MOSER, Stephanie – *Ancestral Images: The Iconography of Human Origins* – p.169 – Cornell University Press (1998)

11. THE IMMORTAL SOUL

1. PLATO – The republic, p. 320 – Everyman (1995)

13. ST JOHN THE BAPTIST

1. (Luke I:80) King James Version
2. (Luke III:3) King James Version
3. ASLAN, Reza – *Zealot* , p.85 – Random House (2013)

14. JESUS

1. OSHO – Living dangerously, pp.124-125 – Watkins (2011)
2. ASLAN, Reza – *Zealot* , p.xxvi – Random House (2013)
3. (Matthew I: 2-16) King James Version
4. (Matthew I: 20) King James Version
5. ASLAN, Reza – *Zealot* , p.26 – Random House (2013)
6. (Romans VIII:13) King James Version
7. (John I:15) King James Version
8. (Mark V:40-42) King James Version
9. (Mark VIII:27-29) King James Version
10. ASLAN, Reza – *Zealot* , p.149 – Random House (2013)

15. ST PAUL

1. (Acts IX: 4-5) King James Version
2. VERMES, Geza – *Christian beginnings: from Nazareth to Nicaea, AD30-325"* pp.26-27 – Penguin Books (2012)
3. ASLAN, Reza – *Zealot* , p.192 – Random House (2013)
4. (Corinthians II: 10-14) King James Version
5. ASLAN, Reza – *Zealot* , p.196 – Random House (2013)
6. (Philippians III: 2) King James Version
7. RUBENSTEIN, Richard E – *When Jesus became God* , p.30 – Harvest Books, Harcourt (1999)
8. (Corinthians III: 6-8) King James Version
9. OSHO – Living dangerously, pp.87-88 – Watkins (2011)
10. (Galatians 3:28) King James Version
11. (Romans X:12) King James Version

16. DID WE NEED A HUMAN GOD?

1. VERMES, Geza – *Christian beginnings: from Nazareth to Nicaea, AD30-325"* p.76 – Penguin Books (2012)
2. VERMES, Geza – *Christian beginnings: from Nazareth to Nicaea, AD30-325"* p.106 – Penguin Books (2012)
3. PAGELS, Elaine – *Beyond belief: the secret gospel of Thomas* - pp.44-45– Pan Books (2003)
4. PAGELS, Elaine – *Adam, Eve and the Serpent: sex and politics in early Christianity* - p. 127 – Vintage Books (1988)
5. DAWKINS, Richard – *The god delusion*, p. 250 – Bantam Press (2006)

6. VERMES, Geza – *Christian beginnings: from Nazareth to Nicaea, AD30-325"* p.55 – Penguin Books (2012)
7. VERMES, Geza – *Christian beginnings: from Nazareth to Nicaea, AD30-325"* p.60 – Penguin Books (2012)

17. ARIANISM, THE COUNCIL OF NICAEA AND THE DEIFICATION OF JESUS

1. RUBENSTEIN, Richard E – *When Jesus became God* , p.56 – Harvest Books, Harcourt (1999)

18. CONSTANTINE AND THE COUNCIL OF NICEA

1. RUBENSTEIN, Richard E – *When Jesus became God* , p.71 – Harvest Books, Harcourt (1999)
2. (Romans X: 4) King James Version
3. RUBENSTEIN, Richard E – *When Jesus became God* , p.56 – Harvest Books, Harcourt (1999)
4. ASLAN, Reza – *Zealot* , pp.213-214 – Random House (2013)
5. VERMES, Geza – *Christian beginnings: from Nazareth to Nicaea, AD30-325"* p.47 – Penguin Books (2012)

21. POSSIBLE CHANGES IN CHRISTIANITY

1. CUPITT, Don – *The meaning of the West – an apologia for secular Christianity* – p.34 – SCM Press (2008)

22. SCIENTISM

1. ANTONELLO, Pierpaolo, *ed.* – Introduction to *Christianity, truth and weakening faith: a dialogue*, p.39 – by Gianni VATTIMO and René GIRARD – Columbia University Press (2010)
2. FROMM, Erich – *The art of loving*, pp. 63-64 – Unwin Paperbacks (1962)
3. DAWKINS, Richard – *The god delusion*, p. 38 – Bantam Press (2006)
4. DAWKINS, Richard – *The god delusion*, p. 19 – Bantam Press (2006)
5. de BOTTON, Alain – *Religion for atheists*, p.11 – Penguin Books (2012)
6. FROMM, Erich – *The art of loving*, pp.61-62 – Unwin Paperbacks (1962)
7. GRAYLING, A C – *The god argument*, p. 108 – Bloomsbury (2013)

8. DAWKINS, Richard – *The god delusion*, p. 31 – Bantam Press (2006)
9. JAMES, Craig A – *The religion virus*, p.192 – O-Books (2010)
10. DAWKINS, Richard – *The god delusion*, p. 165 – Bantam Press (2006)
11. ST AUGUSTINE – *Confessions of a sinner*, p. 47 - Penguin Books – Great Ideas (1961)
12. HOLLAND, Tom – *Dominion – The makking of the Western Mind* – p.523 – Little Brown2019
13. GRAYLING, A C – *The God argument – The case against religion and for humanism*, p. 13 – Bloomsbury (2013)
14. DAWKINS, Richard – *The god delusion*, p. 109 – Bantam Press (2006
15. de BOTTON, Alain – *Religion for atheists*, p.202 – Penguin Books (2012)

23. DARWIN AND THE EVOLUTION OF THE SPECIES

1. UGLOW, Jenny – *Lunar men: the friends who made the future*, p. 270 – Faber and Faber (2002)
2. BUFFON, Georges L L, *Natural History: general and particular... III*, pp.696-697 - U.of Oxford, eBook
3. GREENBLATT, Stephen – *The rise and fall of Adam and Eve*, p.269 – W.W. Norton & Company (2017)
4. DARWIN, Charles – *On the origin of the species*, p.1508 - eBook
5. HOLLAND, Tom – *Dominion – The makking of the Western Mind* – p.425 – Little Brown2019

24. AGNOSTICISM

1. DAWKINS, Richard – *The god delusion*, p. 46 – Bantam Press (2006)
2. WRIGHT, Robert – *The evolution of god*, p.444 – Back Bay Books (2009)
3. HUXLEY, Leonard – *The life and letters of Thomas Henry Huxley* – Volume 1, p.543, eBook
4. HITCHENS, Christopher – *God is not great*, p.275 – Allen & Unwin (2008)
5. ASLAN, Reza – *God: a human history*, p. xiv – Bantam Press (2017)
6. GREENBLATT, Stephen – *The rise and fall of Adam and Eve*, p.2 – W.W. Norton & Company (2017)
7. GREENBLATT, Stephen – *The rise and fall of Adam and Eve*, p.2 – W.W. Norton & Company (2017)
8. WRIGHT, Robert – *The evolution of god*, pp. 5-6 – Back Bay Books (2009)
9. de BOTTON, Alain – *Religion for atheists*, p.12 – Penguin Books (2012)
10. HITCHENS, Christopher – *God is not great*, p.190 – Allen & Unwin (2008)
11. de BOTTON, Alain – Religion for atheists, pp.183-185 – Penguin Books (2012)

12. HITCHENS, Christopher – *God is not great*, p.195 – Allen & Unwin (2008)
13. HITCHENS, Christopher – *God is not great*, p.196 – Allen & Unwin (2008)
14. HITCHENS, Christopher – *God is not great*, p.5 – Allen & Unwin (2008)

26. THE WEST

1. CUPITT, Don – *The meaning of the West – an apologia for secular Christianity* – p.2 – SCM Press (2008)
2. CUPITT, Don – *The meaning of the West – an apologia for secular Christianity* – p.7 – SCM Press (2008)
3. FINKELSTEIN, Daniel – The Times, Wed September 6, 2017 – *Should we care that Britain's lost its religion?*
4. FINKELSTEIN, Daniel – The Times, Wed September 6, 2017 – *Should we care that Britain's lost its religion?*
5. HOLLAND, Tom – *Dominion – The makking of the Western Mind* – p.xxv – Little Brown2019
6. CUPITT, Don – *The meaning of the West – an apologia for secular Christianity* – p.48 – SCM Press (2008)

27. CHRISTIANITY, THE INDIVIDUAL AND THE WEST

1. CUPITT, Don – *The meaning of the West – an apologia for secular Christianity* – p.14 – SCM Press (2008)
2. CUPITT, Don – *The meaning of the West – an apologia for secular Christianity* – p.36 – SCM Press (2008)
3. CUPITT, Don – *The meaning of the West – an apologia for secular Christianity* – p.36 – SCM Press (2008)

28. GOD AS A POSSIBILITY

1. WRIGHT, Robert – *The evolution of god* , p. 4 – Back Bay Books (2009)
2. WRIGHT, Robert – *The evolution of god* , p. 5 – Back Bay Books (2009)

AFTERWORD

1. ANTONELLO, Pierpaolo, *ed.* – Introduction to *Christianity, truth and weakening faith: a dialogue*, p.30 – by Gianni VATTIMO and René GIRARD – Columbia University Press (2010)

2. ANTONELLO, Pierpaolo, *ed.* – Introduction to *Christianity, truth and weakening faith: a dialogue*, p.37 – by Gianni VATTIMO and René GIRARD – Columbia University Press (2010)
3. ANTONELLO, Pierpaolo, *ed.* – Introduction to *Christianity, truth and weakening faith: a dialogue*, p.39 – by Gianni VATTIMO and René GIRARD – Columbia University Press (2010)

www.ingramcontent.com/pod-product-compliance
Lightning Source LLC
Chambersburg PA
CBHW071357290426
44108CB00014B/1581